Rhythm

64 Drills to Live, Lead, and Laugh

Dr. Sven Hansen

Contents

Published by Dr Sven Hansen

PO Box 28-123, Remuera, Auckland 1050;

Copyright © 2022 Sven Hansen

ISBN: 978-0-473-65120-6

Editorial services by Sage Taylor Kingsley, www.SageforYourPage.com

Dedication

To my family:

To Susan, my wife, partner, friend, and best mate, for her steady support and exuberant joy.

To Lauren and James, our children who radiate bounce and flow.

To my brothers, Rob and Tony, who have shared a lifetime of adventure and love.

And to our parents, Joy and John, who provided a wonderful foundation for us all to master our rhythms from inside-out.

Previous books by the author:

Master Stress, 2006

Energise your Body, 2006

Engage Emotion, 2006

Train your Mind, 2006

Spirit in Action, 2006

Inside-out, 2015

Introduction

Life can be perfect. You feel present, vital, connected, agile, and poised in fulfilment. Your life feels rhythmic and strong. Think of rhythm as the music that defines your unique flow throughout the day. Rhythm delivers energy, creativity, and the will to prevail. Life is joyous—a dance.

Life can also be dark and grim. You feel disconnected, fearful, angry, or depressed. Effort seems hopeless. Rhythm is lost. Energy is low. When you lose your rhythm, anxiety and anger collapse into fatigue and depression. The energy and motivation to prevail is weak.

Rhythm is a practical handbook on how you can reduce suffering and increase joy—for yourself, loved ones, work, and the planet.

There is a vast, thriving body of science and practice to help us on the journey with safe, effective, and efficient skills. The goal is to live, lead, and laugh. Peter Koestenbaum argued: "Greatness is the opposite of depression".[1] This perspective has guided my work as a physician and the work we do at The Resilience Institute.

I grew up in a medical family while preventive medicine was just emerging as a field of study. My father, a professor of paediatrics, dedicated his career to improving the wellbeing of children. My mother, a psychiatric social worker, helped restore children from traumatic backgrounds.

During my career assisting people and organisations to apply medicine to foster prevention, boost inner resilience, and enhance wellbeing, it became clear that the simple disciplines covered in this work must be our first step towards living good lives.

Our team has had the privilege of working with thousands of organisations and with hundreds of thousands of people. We have always measured what we do. Our research is available on our website (https://resiliencei.com/)

Rhythm

Our work reduces the symptoms of depression, anxiety, and anger. Our clients learn to Bounce, not back but *forward*, fast. They Grow their physical, emotional, and mental resources. They Connect within themselves, with others, and with nature. Some discover the magic of Flow in sports, work, parenting, nature, or art.

A great life requires dedicated persistence and effort. We live in hyper-stimulated and uncertain times. Threats bombard us. Pressure to succeed is multiplied by the stark suffering of poverty. It is hard enough to shed a few kilograms, let alone master your emotions and control your mind.

Yet a great life is achievable. We can live, lead, and laugh. We each define what that means in our own way. As with any adventure, we need to be well prepared. We must identify and build the skills to master the situations we will face. We need specific fitness elements. A good adventure takes careful preparation. A great adventure takes deep research, deliberate preparation, and practice over time.

Our lives are complex and wonderful journeys. Genetically, evolution has prepared us well. Culture will guide you. Seek the wisdom of your parents and elders. Most importantly, listen deeply for your own rhythms and purpose. Your adventure is unique. It is unfolding in a novel environment. As Alfred North Whitehead famously said: "Becoming is a creative advance into novelty." This truth is ever more relevant in the accelerated, volatile time we find ourselves.

Rhythm is a modern handbook to help you craft your great adventure. Built on strong evidence, proven practices and references, the content is restructured to demonstrate in clear steps how you can Bounce, Grow, Connect, and find Flow. You will learn how to practice drills that enlighten and enrich your life..Be deliberate in testing and fine-tuning the drills. Listen for your rhythm. Dance with it.

Leaders need good maps of the terrain they are leading others through. As a leader, you are responsible for leading people. Ignorance is not an option. Take time for clear understanding.

Dr. Sven Hansen

Mastering your adventure presents many challenges. Each can be solved in many ways and with different tools. Stay alert and test each of the drills in your own reality. Some might work better than others, and at some times more than others.

Subtle ebbs and flows of biochemical energy systems, attention, temperature, sleep, emotion, and movement all feed your rhythm. At times you increase or reduce your pace. This is cadence. With repetition, you will build momentum that carries you forward efficiently. With practice, your drills, rhythm, cadence and momentum create what I call altitude.

When your altitude is low, you become chaotic, rigid, or flaccid. Problems multiply as resources decline. You feel caught in a downward spiral. This leads to feelings of anxiety, anger, fear, and sadness.

When your altitude is high, your rhythm becomes more creative and expressive. Like the musicians in a jazz band, you experience and co-create freedom, flowing from a liberated beat. When you find your rhythm, your experience of life is joyous and fulfilled.

Now, by using the most effective and empowering tools for self-improvement, you will learn to treasure your incredible nature, while also nurturing and accelerating your own evolution. ***By protecting ancient rhythms and building new ones, you can become optimally fit for life, laughter, and leadership.***

At scale, these tools can solve our health crisis—preventable diseases like obesity, diabetes, inflammation, and heart disease can be greatly reduced worldwide. We can counter mental illness. These changes will help our economy, businesses, communities, and families. Thank you for joining me as we create a more resilient planet.

Dr. Sven Hansen, August 2022

Part One: Foundations

The goal of Part One is to lay out the framework, evidence, and attitudes that will help you succeed in your life and leadership. There is no perfect nor agreed upon definition for this work. Be open to different approaches and methods. Pay attention to the language that works for you.

It feels good to find the truth. The scientific method is the most reliable way to test if something is true. We need hypotheses such as: *We can learn to Bounce from depression.* We then test this statement through carefully constructed studies using interventions in different contexts. If researchers can show consistent results, we can conclude that the hypothesis is true. The intervention is trusted to be effective. Truth not only feels good but does good.

Many studies have shown that we can learn to Bounce from depression. In fact, usually we Bounce forward and Grow from the experience. While physical exercise, relaxation practices, nature, positivity, and sleep interventions show increasingly reliable results, the same cannot be said for various creams, supplements, or even antidepressants.[2]

We also want to be sure that the intervention is safe. Poorly executed exercise can cause injury, creams and plastics can alter hormones, drugs have side effects, and even too much sleep causes problems.

Humans are diverse and naturally resilient. While science is a powerful force for good, it is not perfect. There are many paths. Each one of us must consider the evidence, try things out for ourselves, and decide what is best. Be alert and adjust to change. The environment changes, and we change. Solutions must meet the need. Remain curious and exploratory.

The journey starts with waking up to your adventure in *The Call to Action.* Then we investigate the difference between a life that sucks and a life that rocks in terms of *Altitude. Truth and Trust* tests the rigour behind different approaches.

Dr. Sven Hansen

Lead: be a force for Good introduces the idea of altruism as a guiding principle. We can be good and feel good by doing good. We can create a better world, improve the lives of others, and benefit considerably in our own experience. This is leadership.

Strong foundations are essential in uncertain times. Right now, life is edgy. Miracle cures are not the answer. With rational and proven foundations, you reduce suffering and enrich life.

The Call to Action

Drill 1: Fill your tank

1. Sit upright, relax your face, and breathe out slowly through your nose.

2. Stretch your arms behind your back, open your shoulders.

3. Move briskly for a minute—stretch, bounce, walk, or dance.

4. Name three things you are grateful for.

6. Send a pulse of kindness to someone you love.

7. Absorb the beauty of nature, love, or art.

Drill 2: Use your tank deliberately

1. Define one important task for tomorrow.

2. Schedule an hour in your day to complete it.

3. Make sure it is a time of day when you are at your best.

4. Prepare with sleep, exercise, and a good meal.

5. Remove distractions to focus 100% on the task.

Does that work for you? If you want to be productive, you require regular breaks. Perhaps you could build a version of this into each burst of 30 minutes of work. You are creating rhythm.

These rhythm drills are foundational work. Test them, adjust them, and build them into your life. What frequency works best for you? Do you find yourself feeling better afterwards? Where can you build these rhythms into your day?

How did these first two task drills work for you? If you secured and protected the time, you have a win. If you made progress on the task, you are nearly there. If you crushed the task and felt the rush of success, you experienced flow.

Prepare for tasks with renewal. Execute tasks with deliberate intensity. While you feel great afterwards, you burned resources. Only renewal can bring you back to flow. ***Rest, engage, and rest again. Repeat.***

The first goal of this work is to help you find your rhythm. Think of this as pacing, cadence, or momentum. Good work is intense and demanding. You must be well rested and fresh. Performance peaks at specific times of day depending on your circadian (about 24 hours) and ultradian rhythms (about 90 minutes). We address these in detail.

When you nail a burst of success, your recovery and Bounce must be competent and disciplined. Fill your tank efficiently.

Human biology is an almighty orchestra of instruments with multiple rhythms that rise and fall. You, as conductor, must learn to feel and guide these rhythms through your day, week, year, and lifetime.

Rhythm supports the cadence and momentum so you can ride the bumps and surf the waves of life, laughter and leadership. Rhythm supports flexibility, curiosity, and execution.

The second goal of this book is to bring Flow into the adventure that is your life. In the state of Flow, you can increase productivity five-fold.[3] This further delivers success and fulfilment. There is no limit to the different ways you can find Flow in your life.

The third goal of this book is to encourage you to develop specific and practical skills to succeed and to make them intentional and habitual. Anders Ericsson is an authority on expert performance. He is the source of the idea that 10,000 hours of practice lead to expertise. He believes that deliberate practice will trump talent and intelligence every time.[4]

It feels right to believe that natural talent and intelligence will secure success. However, this proves to be wrong. Talent and intelligence can be a liability. It may help us get started, BUT it is deliberate, specific, and focused practice that delivers expert performance.

Pick your battles. Define the drills that work for you. Seek a coach to perfect the drills you need to excel.

The fourth goal of this book is to help you be a force for good. This is to step up to leadership—to work out how you want to impact the world and to do it well. To lead you must master yourself. Build the rhythm, skill, cadence, and momentum to generate life force. Leaders must walk the talk.

As you find that better version of self, your desire to contribute grows. *Leaders define purpose.* What do you want to build or contribute to? Cultivate skills to effect positive change. With hope and courage, you move forward. When you contribute to the positive growth of others, you are a force for good.

Adversity is the crucible of growth. Challenge or adversity stimulates our biology. Change, discomfort, and suffering get our attention. Rather than avoid or protect yourself from the discomfort, listen, learn, and adapt. Growth can be expected. Even in severe personal distress, post-traumatic growth is the most likely outcome.[5] Humans are born to Bounce and Grow. With the right knowledge and drills, positive growth is practically assured.

When we Bounce forward and Grow, Connection and Flow become more likely.

Bounce is learned and perfected. Don't collapse into a fatalistic view that you were either born resilient or you weren't. Evidence shows that we can all learn to Grow and succeed. Emmy Werner's longitudinal

Kauai Study showed that even in the most deprived communities, a third of young people found a way to become competent, confident, and caring adults.[6] Take a deeper look at the study. Although 40 years old, it is proof of growth even in severe adversity. Expect growth.

Our 2022 Research Report shows that in the first quarter of 2020, our global resilience ratios hit a new low. However, by the second quarter resilience was markedly higher than the previous year—and remains high. Whilst the media focuses on the physical and mental health suffering from Covid, the evidence is that it has stimulated Bounce and Growth.[7]

Small, targeted adjustments and investments drive meaningful results.[8]

Your journey is influenced by your genetic inheritance, early upbringing, environmental shaping (epigenetics), culture, and personal effort.

The history of life on this planet is brutal. You had to be strong and adaptive to survive. You are here thanks to evolution. Species that found a way to thrive in the hurly burly of life's lust for itself carved the genetic code that runs through each of us. This is deep inside you and longs for expression.

This ability to Bounce, Grow, Connect, and Flow is embedded in our nature. Each of these abilities has rhythm. Our genes, cells, hormones, organs, and life processes—from digestion and attention to sleep and movement—all have rhythm. Life has rhythm—waves, wind, seasons, day, night, decay, growth, breath, and hibernation's ebb and flow.

Choose an environment that feels good to you. Align your personal rhythms with your environment. Can you feel the music? Can you feel your beat? Are you dancing? Even mental dancing and chair dancing are better than no dancing.

Rhythm

Natural	Biological	Behavioural
Planetary orbits	Sleep	Emotion
Seasons	Digestion	Attention
Day and night	Breath	Speech
Wet and dry	Energy metabolism	Creativity
Growth cycles	Heart-rate variability	Performance

Figure 1: Examples of rhythms

Genes are foundational. Their structure holds the wisdom of our ancestors going back to early life forms. Genetic code is endlessly creative. We mix our genes in each new child. Mutations push forward experiments. Some work and some don't. Farmers and ecologists drive this genetic drift deliberately. They shape the best avocado and breed the best bull.

Genes play a role in muscles, emotional circuits, and attitudes to risk, intelligence, and attention. Genes guide the unfolding of our bodies, emotions, minds, and behaviours. Many a romance holds the potential for new genetic potential. Genes code for rhythm.

Yet, genes are not fixed. Epigenetics shows how we shape our genes. We can change the expression of the DNA in our genes without changing the actual sequence. The environment and state in which we live switches genes on or off. It also protects or damages our genetic code.

For example, genes responsible for diabetes switch on in the presence of refined and processed carbohydrates, and off in lean times. A nurturing family life inhibits the expression of genes that put us at risk of anxiety, depression, and aggression. A destructive family life increases the risk.[9]

It's exciting to know that the environment and lifestyles we choose affect the genes that protect us or predispose us to disease. And these changes to gene expression can cross generations. Distress, poor nutrition, smoking, substance abuse, and inactivity impact the genes of the next generation.

When genetically fortunate people behave badly, their future spirals downward. When genetically less fortunate people behave well, their future shifts upwards.

Your life depends on how you behave—not on what you know or think. Crossing the knowing-doing gap demands deliberate action. It is your personal practices that will have the most impact on your physical, emotional, and mental wellbeing and overall life satisfaction. Lifestyle actions determine 60 to 80% of your life outcomes. For a conservative study from the World Health Organisation read Impact of Lifestyle on Health.

Where and with whom you live and work, what you eat and drink, how you exercise, and how you sleep all have molecular effects on your genetics, physiology, biochemistry, function, structure and experience.

Now let's take a look at the specific practices that will help you empower yourself to create this positive spiral—within you and in your daily life. *Skills and drills* can be grouped into four disciplines: Bounce, Grow, Connect, and Flow.

Rhythm

Bounce

Life includes adversity. It may be self-inflicted or an external force. Be prepared. Humans respond constructively to adversity, finding ways to Bounce, emerge stronger, and be more effective. We learn, adapt, and Grow.

Those who Bounce effectively, focus on what they can achieve rather than blaming others. They maintain and engage supportive networks. They have a bias toward action. Adversity is required to activate these strengths.

The administration of small, repeated shocks might exercise our capacity for Bounce.[10] This has been missing in much modern parenting and education. One can "kill people with kindness".[11] Adversity triggers adaptive responses. As comfort-seeking creatures, we are quick to remove the experience of adversity. Excess safety reduces exploration, medication counters natural healing, tolerance encourages destructive behaviour, and social welfare can undermine resourcefulness.

Mental illness is a crisis of our time. Modern psychiatry, psychology, pharmaceuticals, and safety efforts should have reduced this suffering. Yet despite trillions invested, the suffering continues. While excessive emphases on safety and coddling make us more fragile, they can secure votes and profits.

What if instead of a fear-based, victim-belief-inducing "protect, protect" focus, we could teach Bounce? Might we encourage risk taking? Innovation? Confidence? Boldness? Trust? The risky world humanity is creating has made this a social imperative.

Bounce is base camp.

> ***Bounce forward fast. You cannot Bounce back.***

In adversity you adapt, learn, strive, fail, Bounce, and Grow. This rhythm generates greatness. To achieve your purpose, you must confront and overcome adversity. Bounce is embedded in the heroic journey of history and great literature.

Grow

The second component captures orientation to change, including the daily challenges of life and work. Based on the work *Learned Optimism* by Martin Seligman,[12] we either learn helplessness or optimism. More recently this has been called the Growth Mindset.[13] We can choose to engage constructively and own responsibility for taking the next step.

We Grow through deliberate effort to cultivate physical, emotional, and mental skills, competencies, and reserves.

In learned pessimism (the Fixed Mindset), we believe there is no point trying to engage. We conclude: "I am what I am" and "It is what it is". It feels better to blame external circumstances or others. This victim mindset provokes fear, anger, and sadness. Change becomes a risk to be avoided, fought, or overwhelmed by.

When you take an energised, optimistic, and constructive stance to change and challenge, you Grow. This leads to mastery and success. It stimulates an upward spiral of competence and confidence. Your attention gets focused on your own actions, autonomy, and personal empowerment.

To Grow, you must understand and build your physical, emotional, and mental resources. These are the foundations of success. This is the inner work that enables success externally.

Rhythm

Connect

Connection begins with a respectful engagement with our bodies, our emotions, our thoughts, and our purpose. It extends to family, friends, community, workplace and beyond, to nature and our planet.

Connection requires respect inside and out. It is a measure of maturity—an impulse to goodness. It reflects how we have lived and defines how we will be remembered. Meaningful connection is a responsibility. Mistakes can be expected. They keep you awake.

Provided that you work with self-awareness, respect, tolerance, and altruism,[14] the work of relieving suffering and ennobling others is rewarding at all levels. Your health, emotional state, cognition, and contentment improve when you help others Bounce and Grow.

Targeted, skilful helping is embedded in our evolution. It reaches its finest expression when altruism is practised purposefully.

Here too, there is rhythm. Because to connect and do good, you also have to take care of yourself so you can give and serve from a "full cup". You must make time for rest, reflection, and learning.

And there is a rhythm and balance in how we connect with others, because sometimes others need caring and comfort. Sometimes they need advice, resources, tools, or inspiration. And sometimes they need tough love and a mirror so they can see a truth about themselves and the choices they've been making. Good leaders, coaches, and parents understand how to apply these different influence styles to match the situation.

"

Flow

In flow, our talents and skills rise to meet a relevant challenge. Thinking stops, time stops, we feel effortless grace, and we enjoy a rich afterglow. Flow is expansive and ambitious. It is an altered state where our productivity and creativity are accelerated. It is a source of deep fulfilment.

Evidence shows that those who discover and stretch their talents experience increased life satisfaction, joy, health, and longevity.[15] Aligning our talents and skills with a meaningful challenge enriches life. As we live longer, we have the opportunity to build and enjoy many phases of Flow.

It takes tremendous effort to achieve expert performance.[16] Anders Ericsson showed that thousands of hours of deliberate practice are required. This focused effort must be outside our comfort zone and guided by skilful coaching. Without dedicated effort, Flow is fantasy.

Rhythms of physiology, emotion, mind, and your training drills come together in flow. Up until Flow, one must concentrate deliberately on executing the drill—extrinsic learning. In Flow, it all comes together as intrinsic or embedded learning. Thinking stops and time distorts in an effortless grace. Your symphony is in full Flow.

As conductor of this symphony, it is important that you step back and be able to see how the parts fit together. The job of the conductor is to deliver the performance in flow.

After Flow and a brief celebration, Bounce is required. You must rest, recover, and sleep to fill your physical, emotional, and mental tanks.

You then review your performance to acknowledge your achievements and identify opportunities to learn and improve.

In Grow, we take these learnings and drill them. We adjust, fine-tune, and perfect elements of the performance. We stretch for even greater excellence. Individuals, teams, coaches, and support crew take responsibility for their improvements.

In Connect, we seek to become one with the situation. The body relaxes, heart rate slows, and mind quietens. We feel at one with ourselves. Then we stretch that connection outward to those we serve. We are fully present, calm, open and connected. Through this moment of presence, we step back into Flow.

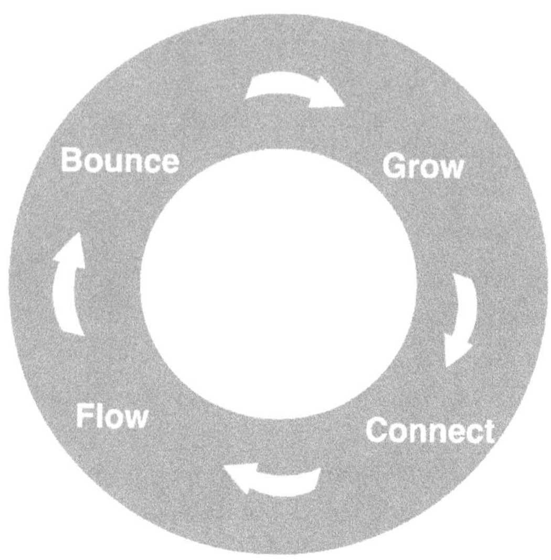

Figure 2: The rhythms of Bounce, Grow, Connect, and Flow

Summary

- Resilience is the learned ability to Bounce, Grow, Connect, and Flow.
- All four will help you, your family, your business, and your community.
- Resilience will relieve pressure on the planet and bring you into constructive engagement with the challenges of the future.

Drill 3: Renewal drills to repeat

1. Sit upright, relax face, exhale slowly through your nose.

2. Stretch your arms behind your back, open your shoulders.

3. Move briskly for a minute: stretch, bounce, walk, or dance.

4. Name three things you are grateful for.

5. Say or send something appreciative to a colleague.

6. Send a pulse of silent kindness to someone you love.

7. Absorb the beauty of nature, love, or art.

In the next chapter, we will learn about altitude and how you can recognise how high you are travelling and what to do to lift your resilience using an evidence-based, integral, and practical framework.

Altitude

Living creatures have good and bad days. We look forward to and appreciate those days when we feel up. We fear and complain about days when we feel low. We say that someone is either a bit low or flying high. This is our altitude. Life has evolved to maintain and increase altitude.

From the earliest bacteria to modern humans, this drive is embedded into our biology. Emotion evolved to support the upward movement. The joy experienced when energised, positive, and engaged is a reward. Life seeks that feeling of joy.

On the other hand, a low day can be marked by distress, pain, fatigue, anxiety, and depression. Life seeks to reduce this discomfort by increasing altitude—more energy, positivity, and engagement. Remember Koestenbaum's statement from the Introduction: "Greatness is the opposite of depression".

Resilience is the learned ability to Bounce, Grow, Connect, and Flow. All four move us up to higher altitudes—away from depression and towards greatness. The work of resilience reinforces life's impulse to move toward joy and away from suffering.

Biological drives are embedded in all creatures. Life needs food, water, warmth, sleep and reproduction. While an organism can be preoccupied with hunting or building a nest, eventually these drives force compliance to the altitude-enhancing impact of food, water, warmth, sleep, and reproduction.

Humans are no different, BUT our creations and willpower confuse the altitude-enhancing drives. We feel hunger and thirst but may satiate them with food and drink that causes disease. Instead of heading up, our consumption drives many of us down. Caffeine, noise, and light inhibit deep sleep so much that health, cognition, and happiness decline dramatically.

Our preoccupations including work, fashion, beauty, devices, and addictive substances are compelling. We seek more—much more. We want it all now. Evolution's drives no longer guide our behaviour strongly. We are free to do what we want. Without the upward force of resilience, we can spiral down into dark places. The evidence is preventable disease, mental illness, and conflict.

Altitude is a conscious guiding insight. If we can notice where we are between greatness and depression, we can take action to move up towards joy.

As we move upwards, energy increases (negentropy). Our lives become more complex, integrated, free, and powerful. We thrive, becoming a force for good in the world. Rhythms emerge. When we spiral down, energy fails (entropy). Our life becomes chaotic, rigid, or flaccid. Life become suffering. Rhythms fail.

Biological energy flows through body, heart, and mind. Few know how to use this resource. It is a gift waiting to be activated. Our wonderful organism is not issued with an instruction manual. This is the mission of this book.

Altitude requires biological insight. By observing the signals from our body, emotions, and thoughts, we perceive the rich dimensions of our life experience. We can connect to body, senses, feelings, thoughts, purpose, and relationships. With training, we can become fully present and effective in every moment.

Take your attention into your body. Notice your posture and muscles. What feels strained and what feels good? Notice your breathing. Follow the flow of air through your nostrils. Watch where the air moves. Follow the change from inhale to exhale and back. See if you can smooth and soften the flow of your breath. Can you feel your heartbeat?

Focus on how you are feeling right in this moment. Can you name the emotions? What thoughts, images, and chatter are going on in your head? Can you bring all of your attention into NOW? Has anything changed as you do this?

Rhythm

Being creative, decisive, and focused in the moment is the experience of Flow. To achieve this state of being, we must understand and master our equipment: body, heart, and mind. This takes time, careful reflection, and practice. Each component, like a symphony, has multiple rhythms.

Altitude is described in our Diagnostic and Development Framework. When we view ourselves through this lens, we bring an integral perspective to our lives. The responsibility is simple and clear.

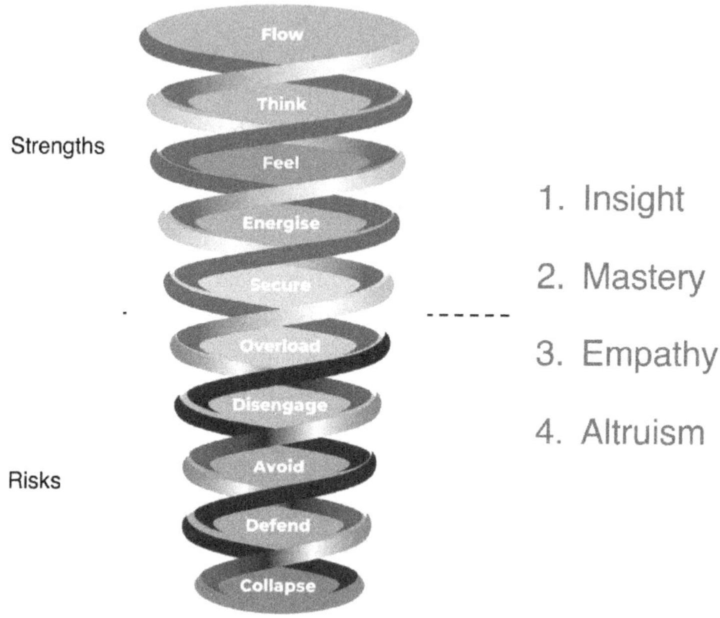

Figure 3: The Altitude Spiral

The framework helps you assess your altitude. One person may be filled with fear, anger, or sadness. Another may be enjoying an outstanding day. This is altitude. Can you discern your level as you examine this spiral?

It is a simplified map of life experience. Each level is called a *category*. While they overlap, each has discrete characteristics that we measure through questions on our Diagnostic. Based on our research and psychometrics, we continuously update and improve the model.

Dr. Sven Hansen

The lower half describes how we lose altitude. Philosophers call it suffering. Scientists use Dissolution and Dysevolution. Physical, emotional or mental distress increases. We call it *resilience failure.* Mind, then emotion, and then body fail progressively. Understanding how this work can encourage us upwards, or at least help us slow a downward spiral until we can regroup and recoup our energy and focus.

The top half shows how to gain biological altitude. Philosophers call this enlightenment. We call it strength or resilience. Life energy expands, choices present, and freedom increases. We learn to fly high. It is a good state to be in. ***The signal is joy.***

Let's explore each category. The bottom half is not comfortable so let's deal with it first. This is our foundation for Bounce and Growth.

Overload is a state of mental confusion and fatigue. There is too much demand on mental resources. We have concentrated too long or switched our attention too often. The mind is exhausted and starts to fail.

Disengage is a state of mental failure. The mind simply drops out of the moment. We go blank, daydream, and lose focus. This is the moment when we surrender human consciousness and wisdom. We are no longer self-directed and responsive. Primitive reactions take hold of our life.

Avoid is the first reaction. We feel unsafe. Doubt creeps in and triggers the emotion of fear. When we fail to resolve this fear, anxiety disorders take hold. In extreme fear, the flight reaction (sympathetic arousal) is triggered.

Defend is the next reaction. Feeling threatened and unable to escape, we default to anger, self-protection and attack. If unresolved, this becomes hostility, aggression, and violence. In extreme anger, fight reactions (sympathetic arousal) are triggered.

Collapse is the final reaction. Overwhelmed, we submit and withdraw. Fatigue and sadness follow. Unresolved, this becomes depression. In extreme situations, freeze reactions are triggered (dorsal vagus nerve activity). We are immobilised, burst into tears, or faint.

Every level or category is a normal, natural, and adaptive response. Evolution has retained flight, fight, and freeze reactions in humans. At times any of these may be exactly what you need. The lower we go, the more we feel suffering. Pain encourages us up. The higher we go, the more we feel joy. Pleasure pulls us upwards.

So, how do we move upwards?

Secure is a state of safety. We experience relaxed trust in the situation. We are fresh, aware, calm, and present. The new (or ventral) vagus nerve is active. Secure is the domain of physiology.

Energise is a state of physical wellbeing. We are rested, fit, nourished, and vital. The body feels alive with boundless energy. Energise is the domain of body, sports science, or preventive medicine.

Feel is a state of emotional resonance. Self-aware, poised, positive, and caring we are connected with ourselves, those around us, and the situation. Constructive feelings support mind and spirit. Feel is the domain of emotion.

Think is being focused and flexible in the moment. Aware, optimistic, agile, and decisive, we have mastered our mind. We are prepared to meet emergent challenges. Think is the domain of mind.

Flow is enlightenment. We are fully engaged with purpose, integrity, altruism, and fulfilment. We have found Flow in life and work. Life is meaningful. Flow is the domain of spirit.

Take time to reflect on your own experience at these levels. Use your own words and stories to help define what each category is like for you. Think about how you perceive others.

Great art, entertainment, or sport can also elicit the feeling of altitude. For example, *Limitless* with Bradley Cooper, Freddie Mercury songs, Wagner, Mozart, or a great tennis final or dance performance.

Practical Application of the Spiral

We can explore the Altitude Spiral from four perspectives: insight, mastery, empathy, and altruism. Each perspective is an opportunity for specific and lifelong practice. We will address specific drills in detail as the journey unfolds. For now, let's understand each lens.

Insight, also called self-awareness, is the ability to look inwards and sense body, emotion, and mind in action. The question to ask yourself is, *Where am I on the spiral?* You can improve your ability to sense your breathing, heart rate, posture, energy levels, emotions, thoughts, and consciousness.

Drill 4: Check body, check emotion, check mind

Mastery, or self-regulation, is the ability to know what to do to improve your position and how to do it. This drill consists of asking yourself a single question: *Where do I need to be now?* Take a moment to ask this inwardly. Watch, listen, and sense because you may get an immediate insight. By asking and being willing to elevate your state, you will learn how to create quick and effective adjustments to your altitude. You achieve this through the skills of Bounce, Grow, Connect, and Flow.

Drill 5: Adjust body, adjust emotion, adjust mind

Empathy, or social awareness, is the ability to tune in to those around us. The question to ask about any social situation is, *How does this look or feel to her/him/them?* Empathy may be focused deeply on one person or expanded to understand the mood of an audience.

Empathy requires considerable biological energy. If we are down the spiral, our focus switches inwards. For example, while you may feel closely attuned to your partner in good times, when conflict erupts, energy is diverted to anger. Empathy shuts down. You may say and do things that you regret. Expanding your empathy by switching your perspective helps you see a deeper, wider truth.

Drill 6: Understand the experience, thoughts, and emotions of others

Altruism, or social skills and leadership, is the ability to interact in a way that helps others be happier, healthier, and successful. The question to ask is, *How can I behave so that he/she feels respected, cared for, and supported to the greatest degree?*

Drill 7: Improve the experience, thoughts, and emotions of others

Insight, mastery, empathy, and altruism are simple to understand but very difficult to master consistently. The earlier you start, the more capable you become. It is never too late. Each lens requires effort, energy, and skill. Each one has rhythm and requires discipline.

An example: At first, I have no idea that I have slumped in the chair during a meeting. As my body slumps, I feel tired and despondent. This sends a 'closed' signal to others. I appear disengaged. Skilful influence in this state is unlikely.

To lead at this level requires energy. Energy is limited so I might work in small steps. Ideally, I would have insight switched on and would notice my posture slump. Immediately, I correct my posture, lengthening the spine and opening the shoulders. This takes physical/muscular effort. I feel better in seconds.

Dr. Sven Hansen

From the open posture, it is easier to attend fully to others. Others notice in real-time. I am more energised, focused, and confident—even my cortisol drops and testosterone increases. I radiate positive impact.

Just as an athlete builds the basics of flexibility, strength, endurance, balance, and speed, you must apply the basics of insight, mastery, empathy, and altruism.

Within each category (or level) are skills to learn and master. Each skill is defined in practical steps so that you can drill those that matter most on your journey up the spiral.

As you begin to master your own rhythms, you will learn to ride the spiral. Enjoy the adventure of clambering up the spiral and finding the confidence, the energy, and the success that awaits you at higher altitudes.

Summary

- Pay attention to your altitude.
- Work the potential of body, heart, mind, and spirit.
- Check your view with insight, mastery, empathy, and altruism.
- Check body, check emotion, check mind.
- Adjust body, adjust emotion, adjust mind.

In the next chapter, we will explore truth and evidence. In a world full of misleading information, you must be able to trust the advice you use. Read on to discover how.

Truth and Trust

Your scepticism is welcome and necessary. We live in complex times and are bombarded with signals to solve our problems by buying this or that. We are inundated with junk—food, supplements, cosmetics, "cures," pills, gadgets, and more.

Do you believe every claim on all the bright, plastic bottles of supplements or cosmetics lining your shelves and screens? How do you decide if they are safe and effective? Multi-trillion-dollar industries have learned to trigger your desires. Most have no good science to support the claims. All we know for sure is that they deliver tons of toxic garbage into our bodies and ecosystems.

As a thought experiment, I recommend that you research the actual benefits and claims made by sunscreens that billions slop over their bodies daily. Tons of toxins enter bodies and ecosystems. Do they work?

Do they protect you from cancer? How do their phthalates affect your hormones? Are you happy to block your testosterone? How do you feel about girls menstruating at nine and boys developing breast tissue? Feel the problem?

Might you simply avoid the midday sun and enjoying a little vitamin D via enriching morning and evening sun? Our ancestors have been doing this for millennia. It works. Vitamin D protects us from disease and improves vitality. There is no skin damage, and we have healthy colour.

As we learn from Covid, should we vaccinate everyone or let immunity develop naturally as it has for billions of years? People have strong views. What is true? Who can you trust?

Most of us know someone ensnared in the paranoid echo chambers of social media. We care about them, and yet their beliefs have become so extreme and polarized that conversation and compromise are no longer possible.

Dr. Sven Hansen

Humans are gullible. Our brains shape our perception of reality to help our minds make sense of experience. We use stories to simplify complexity. Advertising knows how to manipulate our emotions. Quick success without risk is promised.

It is clear that our impulsive consumption poses an intimidating risk to humanity and Planet Earth. Obesity, diabetes, mental illness, inflammation, myopia, inequality, debt, and looming environmental catastrophe all creep up slowly on us. So slowly that we fail to notice. Remember the boiled frog analogy? Throw the frog in hot water, and it leaps out. Heat the water slowly, and it slowly boils to death. We have many boiling frogs in the pot. A healthy child develops puppy fat, then a teenage belly, and 'suddenly' a diagnosis of obesity or diabetes.

The same is true of global warming and mental illness.

Some people are stepping up to these challenges despite the cynical neglect of most governments. One must admire their commitment and tenacity. Some devote their lives to defeat the threats. Bravo. It is hard work, often thankless, and sometimes depressing. We have known about climate change for nearly forty years. Only now are we slowly responding. The climate forcing we have initiated will continue to play out for a thousand years.

Some stick their heads in the sand and ignore the issues entirely. They distract themselves with more trivial concerns. Or there are times— exams, working or aging parents, young children, business difficulties, divorce, financial loss, or illness—when personal matters are all you have energy for.

Some make it their mission to actively deny the emerging threat. Usually, there is an industry ready to profit from denial. Some examples: *Soft drinks don't cause obesity. Climate change has nothing to do with coal. Social media is not causing mental illness. Guns don't kill, it is mental illness.* Industries behind the problem are quick to fund and support the claims—and pocket the profits.

Rhythm

The skill and tenacity with which the fossil fuel industry has denied both the science and the risk of carbon emissions for over thirty years is remarkable. Lobbyists spend billions distorting truth and delaying ethical action. They attract and enlist a mob of angry and noisy denialists who make it their life purpose to promote mistruths.

Every view has its own claim to truth. Yet today, thankfully, truth can be tested. The role of science is to apply reason, disciplined method, and practical experiments to challenge or prove an idea. If the idea can be proven repeatedly in different situations, we can begin to trust it as true.

Science makes errors. Scientists can be greedy, celebrity-seeking charlatans. Increasingly, they get found out. And even the most brilliant scientists and doctors, while recommending exercise, fail to do it themselves. We are not as smart as we like to think.

Magical thinking continues to drive downright stupid decisions and behaviours. Many confidently deny evolution, vaccines, climate change, and the moon landing. It makes us human. Yet these erroneous beliefs can cause terrible suffering.

A refreshing read is Dan Lieberman's *Exercised*.[17] He carefully explores how three quarters of humanity manage to avoid the one practice that has 100+ years of bulletproof evidence. If you want to beat heart disease, cancer, diabetes, obesity, dementia, osteoporosis, osteoarthritis, anxiety, depression, sleep disorders, and death, 150 minutes of activity per week does it best.

If you want to be calm under pressure, experience vitality, master emotion, train your mind, increase libido, and take more holidays, simply exercise 150 minutes a week. So clear, so direct, so obvious, so inexpensive, so potentially enjoyable and tremendously rewarding, and yet *most* of humanity avoids the practice.

Build your own truth, establish trust, then get clear, and get in gear. These principles can help you avoid painful mistakes.

Dr. Sven Hansen

Be Evidence-Based

Scientific method, by seeking truth, has improved life dramatically. When you switch a light on, remember how hard it is to light a fire in a rainstorm. When you take an antibiotic, remember what it would be like to have a limb amputated. Science has transformed our experience of life.

Resist wild promises that require no effort. Press for good evidence before adopting a practice or advocating it for others. Cultivate hope and optimism that things can change for the better. Make science work for a better world.

We are in a biological worldview. It is the foundation of all life, healing, and performance sciences. Biology is a systems science that integrates complexity. Evolution, ecology, medicine, sports science, and epidemiology are biological. The social sciences such as psychology, anthropology, and sociology are scrambling to replace outdated theories with biological foundations.

Life is not hard science. Life is experience—a subjective perspective. No matter how detailed our understanding of a certain emotional process may be, we cannot describe that subjective experience from a brain scan. To do this requires listening, understanding, and shared experience.

This is why we must respect subjective experience. While molecules, neurotransmitters, neural firing, and convergence zones most certainly underpin the experience of love, they are not love.

Run your own experiments. If you like an idea and feel confident in the claim, try it out. If it works, it is successful. Perhaps it is placebo effect. That's OK. Use it generously. If you believe in the remedy, that belief will help you get benefits.

Rhythm

Be Integral

Living is a complex process. People love a simple solution. Scientists study increasingly narrow fields. The expert in creative dream (REM) sleep rarely has much understanding of other physical, emotional, and cognitive fields, let alone other aspects of sleep. Watch out for the "expert" who recommends that you just take this one pill, cream, or course.

The better version of yourself requires the integration of different perspectives. Yes, broccoli is good. So is variety. Add a touch of fitness and a good night's sleep, and the broccoli is optional. Add impulse control and positivity, and broccoli might be trivial.

Integral means we never forget the different physical, emotional, cognitive, and spiritual aspects of our life. Admittedly, this is hard. It is easier to embrace the benefits of a broccoli fad. Charlatans know this well. *If you just follow my one amazing trick (supplement, food, diet, exercise, breathing, etc.), everything in your life will improve!*

To be integral requires a wide focus—an ability to step back and ask what you are missing. A mere hundred years ago, our grandparents only had the experience of one culture, one religion, and one way of life. Today we live alongside many cultures, religions, and lifestyles. We can be experts in multiple cultures and religions and choose solutions that take the best of each.

An integral approach allows you to switch perspective between the physical, emotional, and cognitive. It allows you to understand and respect the many different belief systems with respect. Being integral heals our sometimes narrow and judgmental echo chambers. This is the foundation of maturity and wisdom.

Dr. Sven Hansen

Be Practical

Good science must be translated into clear, actionable steps. We can ramble on about the benefits of high intensity training, but if we cannot action something practical, it is distracting noise. You must find ways to close the knowing-doing gap.

Knowledge must become action. If the action is effective, knowledge grows and becomes real. Deliberate, focused, and regular practice leads to skill and then expertise. With expert skill, we work up the resilience spiral.

A healthy digestive system, strong muscles, deep sleep, calm, positivity, focus, agility, and Flow all require deliberate, alert repetition over time. Deliberate means that your skill is well defined, flexible, and repeatable in a range of situations. Alert means that you are paying attention to what you are doing. You are not lost in daydreaming or distraction. Most of us need skilled coaching to secure expertise. Personalized feedback from a coach, video analysis, or biofeedback accelerates our learning and skill acquisition.

We cannot wait for all the facts before acting. The human mind is equipped to make decisions without full information. We use experience and emotional judgement to decide, and course correct as we go. Life is action. If a certain practice makes sense, try it. In time, you learn to recognise the practices that change your biology (through direct, subjective experience) for the better. Use them and fine-tune them as more data comes to hand.

No community has yet engaged the full power of modern biology. This is an exciting opportunity and emerging reality. More and more people will live to 100 and more. Many will stay physically and economically competitive well into their eighties and nineties. Stay open to this possibility. Imagine being part of a community that takes biology—and rhythm—seriously, supporting all members in their journey up the spiral.

Rhythm

Biology is a living science. It is growing and maturing at an extraordinary pace.

The goal is positive subjective experience. This experience emerges from what we do—our daily practices. Aligning our practices with carefully considered principles can lift your game and simplify decision-making.

Clarify your principles and refine your practices. We support this effort with the best evidence we can find and the experience of those who have tested the limits.

The scientific approach can help us find the most logical and effective means to achieve our goals. The real test is in your life—body, heart, mind, and spirit. Science still has a lot to discover. Don't wait. Get started now.

Tackle the journey in bite-size chunks. Read a section at a time, and if the practice seems relevant, stop, work out how to take some action and experiment. Get help where and when you need it.

Study! Practise! And if you feel the urge, teach!

Summary

- Be sceptical.
- Biological understanding is accelerating very fast.
- Be evidence-based, integral, and practical.
- Close your knowing-doing gap.

Next up is how to be an effective force for good. There are many challenges facing humanity and wonderful opportunities to build the resilience of others. We call this altruism or leadership.

Dr. Sven Hansen

Lead: Be a Force for Good

As we struggle through the valleys, deserts, and thickets of life, two towering mountains beckon from above the clouds.

The first is the peak of self-importance. The gleam of wealth, power, immortality, and fame motivates us up to the foothills to start the climb to personal power.

The second is the peak of altruism or benevolence. We climb it to make a positive difference to our world and the sentient beings that share it. This path is more challenging. The benefits are less obvious. In fact, as you progress, the hazards and difficulty increase. Entrepreneurs who start with vision and enthusiasm, discover the hardship required to lead a business and manage people. Deciding to have children is noble. Raising them well is a demanding journey.

Owning your rhythm of resilience and wellbeing prepares you for the summit of both peaks. We must master ourselves before we define and follow our true purpose. We practice on the first peak (self-mastery) to help us up the second (altruism and leadership).

On the second peak, our purpose contributes to the health, happiness, and success of others. This is complicated, ambiguous, and demands sacrifice. Yet it is the most rewarding rhythm of all. We work on ourselves to serve others better. This is leadership.

It is not a sin to focus on your own needs. To secure an education and build a career demands focus. At times we may have to attend to our health. The risk is becoming self-absorbed. Self-absorption reduces our desire to contribute. The goal, often at any cost, is to be famous and worshipped. It is fed by a need for approval. This is the narcissist.

To have not-for-profit or community experience on your CV is fashionable. The work is a way to build interest and desire for good. Whilst self-serving, it does direct energy towards serving others. As the wealthy compete for who gives the most, resources can be shifted in helpful ways. With clear thinking and professional support, philanthropists do incredible work.[18],[19]

Some serve others with such commitment that they neglect themselves. Helping others feels good. Yet if we neglect ourselves, we cannot give others the skilled support they need. You may experience this when you visit a doctor who is clearly not able to take care of himself. Or the exhausted mother desperately serving family whilst neglecting her own needs. Or the workaholic professional developing more and more physical and mental health problems.

Parenting can leave us too exhausted and fragile to parent effectively. Many professionals are so compromised that their ability to make decisions—let alone lead people—is severely compromised.

Drill 8: Take care of yourself

1. First, take care of yourself.

2. Second, before you set out to help others, take care of yourself again.

3. Third, if you are helping others, take care of yourself in a disciplined and ongoing way.

The impulse to help others is a step in the right direction, but it can have unhelpful consequences. Imagine you pass a beggar on the street. You feel an urge to help. Look deeper and you feel massive discomfort within yourself. This ugly feeling of pity and guilt is empathic distress.

If you give the beggar a coin, empathic distress is quickly relieved. You can hold your head high as a generous person. You feel much better and continue on your way.

But have you helped the beggar? Did your coin secure a rush of nicotine, alcohol or worse? Has the beggar Bounced, Grown, Connected, or found Flow? Will they be better off tomorrow? Or still sitting in a miserable heap waiting for you? When empathy collapses into empathic distress (sympathy), you help no one.[20]

To guide or lead others to a better, higher altitude is very difficult. It is the drama of parenting, teaching, and leadership. A child is sad, so give them a sugar rush. Feels good now but the consequence of obesity and diabetes causes chronic suffering for millions. Your patient complains of pain. Be a good doctor and prescribe relief. Feels better now but how do you overcome an opioid crisis that has over 10 million addicted and killed over 100,000 in the US last year?

As discussed in *The Call to Action*, Twenge, Haidt and Lukianoff demonstrate how anxious and permissive parenting leads to isolated, anxious, and depressed young adults. Parents, educators, and leaders have the best intentions. They are kind, generous, helpful, and loving. If, in the desire to help and keep safe, we take away responsibility, how do young people and workers learn to Bounce and Grow?

Empathic Distress—sympathy or kindness without restraint and wisdom—can constrain, cause harm, and even kill. As the old proverb (possibly from Lao Tzu) goes: "Give a man a fish and you feed him for a day; teach a man to fish and you feed him for a lifetime."

It is much easier to give the fish away. This happens in education, welfare, human resources, and government. Handouts, without the support to build skills, can leave millions without the life skills to fend for themselves.

Being a force for good is complex and demanding. You must be high on the spiral. Secure first your own ability to Bounce, Grow, Connect, and Flow.

Every time you let your altitude drop, you lose energy, succumb to impulse, and make poor decisions. So, if you are a caregiver, parent, coach, teacher, leader, or a social entrepreneur, please take very good care of yourself before you do anything else.

Then we must be humble. We are playing God in a system where evolution has ruled for billions of years. We are interfering in profound ways. Humanity must learn to respect and address both the short- and long-term consequences of our actions.

We are struggling to address this uncomfortable topic. Environmental forces press on living systems. Those that adapt successfully thrive. Those that fail, disappear. Thus, the gene pool of each species is shaped to survive and flourish in its niche. The hunters become ever more deadly. The hunted ever more evasive.

Humanity now manipulates those environmental forces with great power and little responsibility. We have unleashed a tsunami of environmental forcing, with profound and deadly consequences.

We poison, plunder, and deplete our oceans. We fill our atmosphere with pollution that kills millions every year. We force climate into unstable change. We drive the loss of biodiversity. The survival buffer of ecosystems is deeply scarred.

We cannot stop ourselves.

The investment in products and services that undermine our current and future wellbeing is startling. There is no limit to the creativity devoted to preventing exercise, delivering junk food to our lips, serving every impulse with a swipe, and disrupting our natural human requirements for sleep, nature, movement, touch, and emotional connection.

Daniel Lieberman,[21] an anthropologist, talks about the explosion of preventable *mismatch diseases* or *dysevolution*. He describes how lack of activity is causing our foot bones to fuse, how fitness declines, life-threatening obesity and diabetes become normal, and how our jaws and mouths have shrunk to the point that breathing is compromised. Myopia (short-sightedness) has exploded as we stare at our screens from within confined spaces. Lockdowns amplified myopia.

Stephen Porges,[22] a neurophysiologist, talks about the *dissolution* of our nervous systems. He argues that we evolved our new vagus nerve pathways to feel calm, safe, and connected. Today we have an explosion of anxiety, autism, attention disorders, hostility, and depression. He explains how this is a return to more primitive states of flight, fight, and freeze. More on this later.

As we shape our environment to immobilise, constrain, digitise, protect, and isolate, we drive an epidemic of preventable disease and suffering. Parts of humanity are deep into dysevolution (or dissolution).

On the other side of the divide are nurturing families, who are educated, employed, and actively shaping their evolution in positive directions. Skilfully applying fitness, nutrition, sleep, emotional intelligence, and mental skills, these households and communities accumulate wealth, influence, freedom, and resilience.

For most of evolution, natural selection prevented this wealth and health gap. The spread of a species was defined to a reasonably tight bell curve (or normal distribution). Our human bell curve is widely spread and multimodal across a range of measures including wealth, health, productivity, fertility, and longevity.

As we become more proficient in engineering solutions, we will become increasingly forceful in shaping evolution. We could shape individuals and communities in wonderful and positive ways. When we watch the Olympics or great theatre, we are in awe of the performers and performance. We feel the rhythm and flow.

On the other hand, as we get to understand the scale of suffering caused by obesity, mental illness, and dependency, we feel despair. Rhythm fades.

We have the resources to shape the evolution of humanity with skill. This is the purpose of the Resilience Institute. As we reduce suffering and build the physical, emotional, and mental resources of people and community, we can liberate lives, restore communities, and build momentum to become better stewards of our planet.

Resilient people forge the path to a resilient planet.

It is always a good time to be good. Humanity faces many risks and real challenges confront the workforce. There are tantalising opportunities to make life so much better. We have the knowledge and tools. We can be a force for good. Yes, it is complex. Creativity and patience will be required. Remain humble and courageous.

The spiral below guides you as a skilful force for good. Secure your own altitude. You need this altitude to comprehend and solve the challenges to individuals, community, fellow species, and our planet.

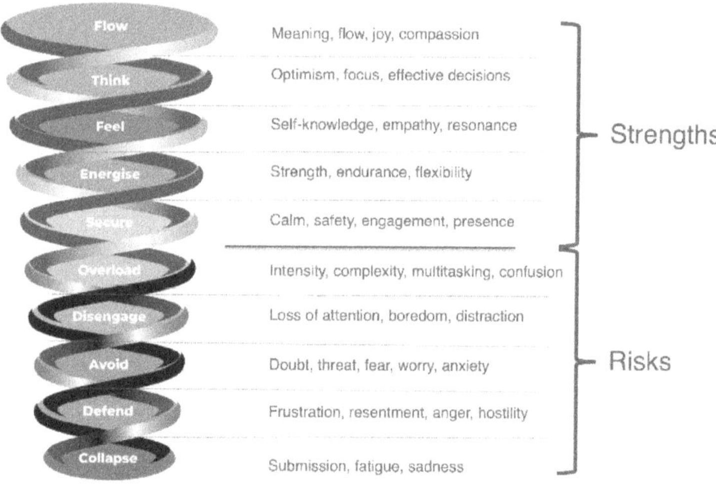

Figure 4: The Resilience Spiral (Individual)

From the right altitude, we can perceive, comprehend, and engage with altruism. With wisdom, compassion, and skill, we can identify where we can make our best contributions. Some may choose to relieve suffering through counselling. Perhaps, you become a psychologist or psychiatrist to help individuals and families. Maybe you contribute to community projects that develop skills and basic services. Others may choose to contribute to higher levels of achievement. Perhaps this could be coaching athletes or leaders. Perhaps it is building resilient culture at work.

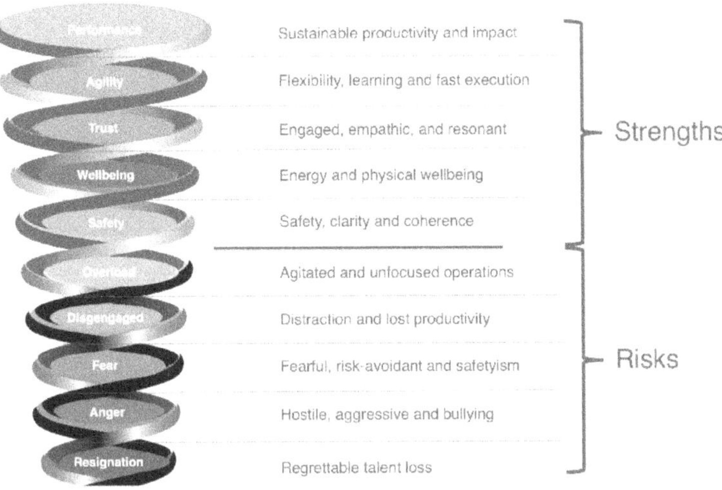

Figure 5: The Resilience Spiral (Leadership and Culture)

The two models shown above are essential frameworks to understand the role of leadership—or being a force for good.

Keep an eye on integral interactions. Yes, an ice-cream feels good. Is obesity and diabetes a reasonable risk to take? Weigh up the short-versus long-term effects of your actions. Comfort and nurturing may be appropriate. At other times, firm and authoritative parenting or coaching may deliver better results.

Here are some examples of how you may become a force for good.

Rhythm

With mental illness increasing, **Bounce skills** are in high demand. Anxiety, depression, autism, and attention disorders cause terrible suffering. Perhaps you might help young people understand and master Bounce in these conditions.

With sedentary, machine-aided lives we must create ways to **enhance our physical, emotional, and thinking capacities**. To meet the economic challenges of today, we can no longer rely on genes or survival pressures. Would you be interested in helping others understand how to cultivate and expand capability? Physical activity, positivity, and attention have transformative effects on wellbeing.

When communicating through a screen, we must be deliberate in the **skills to Connect—self-regulation, empathy, and influence.** While smart software is good, it cannot beat a collaborative team. Both young and old can benefit from the social and emotional intelligence required for creativity and collaboration.

What about helping others to **find Flow**? If we support, coach, and sometimes challenge others to apply skills to a task, we can help them achieve their goals and realise a meaningful life. What could be more rewarding?

Humans have come a long way. Violence has been on the decline since 1300. Slavery is mostly gone. Many diseases have been eradicated. Poverty has halved. Life expectancy has nearly doubled. Most men and women have finished primary school. Over 80% are vaccinated and have electricity.[23]

We have the energy, time, and capability to achieve way more than at any other time in our evolution. The playing field is tilted strongly towards enlightenment. Good (or God) can win.

You feel good when you Bounce, Grow, Connect, and Flow. You feel even better when you nudge others to Bounce, Grow, Connect, and Flow as well.

To succeed, we must resolve the tension between cynicism and optimism. Philosopher Bertrand Russell taught that a good life was inspired by love and guided by knowledge.[24] In *Human Kind*,[25] Rutger Bregman beautifully challenges us to reframe the entrenched idea of human selfishness by examining our goodness. His central thesis is that we are 'friendly, peaceful and healthy'.

Human institutions including religion, philosophy, medicine, law, science, and government have altruism at their core. All too often, they lose their way in seeking dominance, wealth or fame. Many institutions are lost in a world long past. We need new institutions, and they are emerging in creative ways.

Many paths can take us forward. We must seek the one that suits best. Minimum harm, measurable effectiveness and efficiency must be kept in mind.

Summary

- Be in the best possible state.
- Resist impulsive sympathy in the face of suffering.
- Consider the unique situation of the person you wish to help.
- Reflect on the longer-term outcomes.
- Lay out your options and choose your interventions carefully.
- Execute skilfully.
- Just in case you forgot, take care of yourself.

Next up is the critical role of Bounce. Let's dive into how you can understand the effects of adversity and learn how to Bounce.

Part Two: Bounce

The goal of Part Two is to counter adversity with growth and wisdom. To succeed we must welcome adversity, assess it accurately, and Bounce forward fast. These chapters address the mental health crisis directly. To solve it—and we can—understand suffering and master it with expertise.

Mental health challenges are often part and parcel of great leadership, creativity, personal transformation, and art. Emotional and intellectual ups and downs are normal rhythms that life has retained through evolution for our own good. To catastrophise mental illness, bombard it with drugs, and overprotect people from adversity, is a failed strategy.

Do you want to be coddled and protected from every tussle with adversity? Or do you prefer to experience the full and scary adventure of life? Will you welcome adversity and pain as stimuli for growth and wisdom?

Both views have merit. We want to take care of our children, and we also want our children to learn how to manage adversity and be resourceful adults. If we remove all adversity, they remain fragile and vulnerable. Leadership confronts the same tension between performance and care, risk and caution.

Life will present serious challenges. It is inevitable that we stumble. When we do, we want to Bounce—not backward to the past but forward into a more resourceful state. This confidence and ability to Bounce forward in the face of adversity stimulates Growth, Connection, and Flow. It is the great rhythm in life: the Hero's journey.

We can get much better at helping young and old towards rapid Bounce, skilled recovery and calm presence in times of challenge.

Embrace the Challenge describes the nature of challenge and how evolution has set us up to deal with adversity. *Resilience Failure* explains how resilience can fail. When you understand and detect adversity, the work of Bounce already has begun. *Bounce Forward Fast* is a practical guide on how to Bounce forward fast. *Tactical Calm* provides a range of practical solutions for remaining calm, controlled, and connected regardless of the pressure.

To understand and master Bounce is the foundation of human greatness.

Embrace the Challenge

The purpose of this chapter is to understand and master how you respond to pressures, challenges, and threats.

Your goal is to implement a skilful and successful response. It is rewarding. Think about those great leadership or sporting moments when you mastered adversity. A destructive reaction can be ugly. Take time to examine how you react to challenges. Ask: *What happened?* This deepens your insight.

With insight, we understand, learn, and master. When we understand our reaction, we can learn to master a better response. This learning is far superior to avoidance or medication.

What happens when you confront an acute threat? Does it provoke an upsetting reaction or a skilful response? The answer defines your resilience. When you react badly, life gets messy. When you respond well, life improves. You Bounce, Grow, Connect, and Flow.

Nature can deliver shocking trauma. People can be rude and nasty—in class, amongst friends or family, in traffic, in a store, or at the office. Our muscles tighten, our stomach churns, and the world closes in. Our heart accelerates, our blood pressure increases, adrenaline spikes the body, and nor-adrenaline floods our brain.

When threatened, we can react with primitive reactions. In flight, we feel fear that drives us to retreat, lie, or run away. In fight, we feel anger that drives us to shout, swear, or hurt. In freeze, we feel overwhelmed or bullied and can collapse, cry, or submit. We have lost our rhythm and become chaotic, rigid, or flaccid.

We all experience times when bad situations have trapped us in these ancient reactions. On reflection, it is clear to see that they rarely achieve our aims.

Drill 9: Define unhelpful reactions to difficult challenges:

1. Fear and flight reactions: avoid, retreat, lie, or leave the room

2. Anger and fight reactions: shout, swear, or strike out to hurt others

3. Sadness and freeze reactions: withdraw, submit, cry, collapse, or faint

---

Examples include being attacked or bullied, stopped by police, speaking in front of an audience, cut off in traffic, a natural disaster, conflict in an important relationship….

Examine your own life. Sometimes these are just uncomfortable challenges— worry about a test or speech—and we can quickly move on. At other times, we might react really badly—perhaps in an argument— and we can end up walking out (flight), shouting (fight), or bursting into tears (freeze).

Life unfolds one situation at a time. ***When reaction trumps response, suffering follows***. Resilient rhythms are lost. These situations have a process:

1. A trigger event, word or behaviour
2. An immediate reaction
3. Destructive fear, anger, or sadness
4. Regret upon reflection.

When you learn to respond with skill, life improves—one response at a time. This skill is also called impulse control. With it, rhythm is restored.

Look at your destructive reactions with courage and candour. If you conclude that something you did was unhelpful, you explore it to understand what happened. Then you begin the work of learning to respond with skill.

To learn how to respond to a challenge, identify specific challenges to work on. What was the trigger? What happened? What would have been a better response? Then address these situations with more skill. Take the tricky situations in your life and turn them into interesting and deeply rewarding opportunities to Bounce, Grow, Connect, and Flow.

Create a list of three challenges in your life where you want to respond better:

Describe the challenge	Describe your reaction	What would work better?

Figure 6: Replacing reactions with better responses

For any challenge, we can measure our response or reaction. How we react or respond defines our resilience.

Dr. Sven Hansen

Let's say someone attacks you for poor performance. There are five zones of response as shown in the diagram below. The model is adapted from David Grossman, *On Combat.*[26] It originated as the Yerkes-Dodson Curve in 1908.

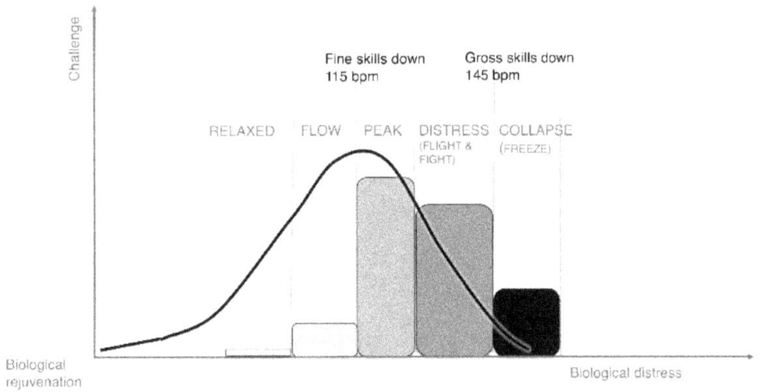

Figure 7: Reaction to Challenge Curve

1. Relaxed: You remain relaxed and passive. While you don't get upset, you're also not motivated to deal with the situation. Sometimes you must pick your battles.
2. Flow: You become alert, focus your mind, and engage calmly and effectively. This takes practice. This is the best way to engage a challenge. It produces results and respect.
3. Peak: You get a shock, feel the adrenaline, your body tenses, and you respond rapidly and perhaps aggressively. You storm into the argument with guns blazing. You are too activated to listen and execute well. At times, you can use this in short bursts.
4. Distress: You feel pressure and upset. As your sympathetic system activates, your heart accelerates, your breathing tightens, and you feel anxious (flight) or angry (fight). It is very hard to respond effectively. People will notice your distress and discomfort.
5. Collapse: You are overwhelmed and submit. You react by collapsing in the situation (freeze). You submit, burst into tears, or even faint.

Rhythm

Note how in this version of the curve, the dominant reactions are peak, distress, and collapse.

This curve is often called the stress curve. Stress is confusing. Do you mean stress out there in the world or in your body? Do you mean good stress (eustress) or bad stress (distress)? Challenge or pressure is a more precise name for external demand. Using the five categories of reaction is a precise way to name the internal state.

If you want to Bounce, Grow, Connect, and Flow, you must practice dealing with distress. Move your biology from distress to Flow as fast as possible.

Drill 10: Insight into the situations you described

1. Define the trigger event (the straw that broke the camel's back).

2. Describe your reaction or response (flow, peak, distress, failure).

3. Name the emotion: fear, anger, sadness, or craving.

4. Detail what others experienced: What did they see, hear, feel, or think?

5. What was the result of your reaction or response?

> **Drill 11: Deepen your biological insight**
>
> Map your reaction to each of the three situations.
>
> Try to remember your biology.
>
> Can you remember if your heart accelerated?
>
> How did your body move?
>
> What happened to your breathing?
>
> How did you feel? Can you name the emotions?
>
> Can you remember what you were thinking?
>
> How did you respond?
>
> What exactly did you say or do?

The more you study your reactions in edgy situations, the more opportunities you will discover to respond with skill and expertise. This is situational awareness: check body, check emotion, and check mind.

When you understand what happened, you will want different outcomes. Mastery is your next step.

There are four steps to master a skilful response:

1. Practise restraint: pause and name your feelings.
2. Breathe out: relax your face and shoulders.
3. Respond and engage with calm, empathy, honesty, and purpose.
4. Be calm and positive in serious adversity and crisis.

You can start with simple restraint. It is a big, empowering step. Life starts to improve. When you can name what you are feeling, you are in a position of heightened insight and choice. By using a method to relax into the moment, you are on the threshold of mastery. Your life is getting better.

Prepare carefully and rehearse in safe, practice situations. Secure good sleep, sensible nutrition, breath control, fitness, and good posture. We address all these in later chapters.

There is rhythm in our response to challenge. We awaken to the opportunity, soften to engage effectively, execute with precision, relax, and move on. Life and leadership improve.

Perform under Pressure[27] by Ceri Evans is a good read to master those critical pressure moments that lead to world-class performance. The model is simple and clear. It has been effectively applied by the All Black rugby team who have dominated rugby for many years.

1. Red (destructive emotion) or blue (calm insight)
2. Decide (choose reaction or response)
3. Do (step into the situation and execute with purpose)

Drill 12: Plan to master an edgy challenge

Clarify how you want to respond to that situation.

Visualise yourself responding in the right zone: relaxed, Flow, or peak.

Prepare for the situation with a colleague or friend.

Plan for the situation carefully. Where, when, how, what.

Review your performance and select the next improvement.

Drill 13: Apply deliberate practice with focused repetition

Pick a situation to become expert at. Drill the solution every day for six weeks.

If it is conflict, seek out difficult people and tricky situations. Drill.

If it is anxiety in your sport or exams, seek high pressure situations. Drill.

If it is fatigue, leap out of bed ahead of your alarm. Drill.

If it is snacking or gorging, say no. Eat lean one day a week. Drill.

If it is exercise, start now with 5 minutes of brisk walking. Drill.

You are mastering your response to challenge. Distress and failure will transform into Flow and relaxation. You are mastering the engage-relax rhythm of life. Your day becomes more playful and fluid. The chaos of anxiety, rigidity of anger, and flaccidity of sadness drop away. Secure, calm, and agile responses unfold with increased frequency and ease.

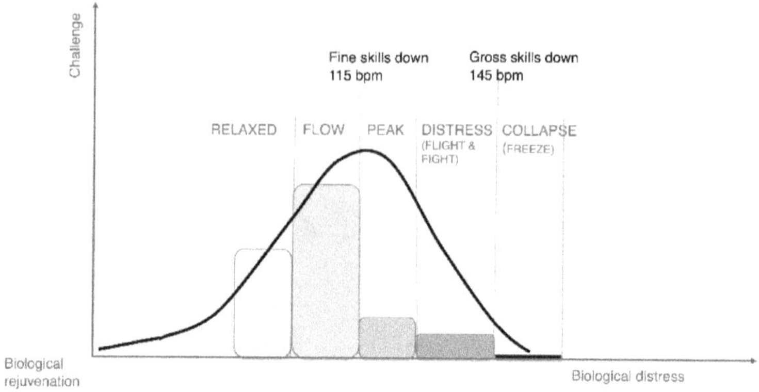

Figure 8: A balanced and skilled response profile under pressure

Above we can see a better profile. The challenge is the same but now the person responds with more relaxation and Flow, and with much less peak, distress and failure. This person still rises to peak when needed. This is the rhythm of response to challenge that leads to Flow.

Gillian, a CEO I am currently coaching, has found this transformational. She has used it to move from crippling fear to tackling challenges as an adventure. It has helped her reconnect and re-engage through a difficult leadership period.

Simply checking your heart rate, blood pressure, or breathing rate will reveal your reaction or response to a challenge.

We will address these tools in more depth in future chapters. Remember the foundation drill on page 1? You can use this right now to get deeper into Flow with whatever challenge faces you.

Summary

- ☐ Define the challenges that matter to you.
- ☐ Understand your reactions and responses.
- ☐ Practice restraint, relaxation, and skilful engagement.
- ☐ Nurture the rhythm of your engage-relax cycles.

Now you understand how humans react or respond to challenge, the next chapter addresses how resilience fails—your foundation for Bounce.

Resilience Failure

The purpose of this chapter is to help you recognise how your resilience fails.

We face a global pandemic of anxiety, depression, conduct disorders, autism, and attention disorders. Despite massive investments in prevention, diagnosis, and treatment, we are losing this battle.

The problems are complex. Mental illness, along with diabetes, obesity, and sleep disorders are what Professor Dan Lieberman calls mismatch diseases.[28] Modern lifestyles disrupt the natural rhythms that support us. As these rhythms collapse, the door to suffering opens.

Biology can help us solve the mental-health drama. Evolution has given us the tools to deal with adversity: Bounce, Grow, Connect, and Flow. We must use them with wisdom. When you understand what happens in adversity, you will Bounce faster.

Things will go wrong. Adversity strikes through a difficult event, bad luck, or our own bad choices. We are knocked down. Resilience fails. We feel distress. Bounce, Grow, Connect, and Flow are hard to imagine at this time.

Let's explore some examples.

Angie's friends are the most important part of her life. A new girl comes into the group who is jealous of Angie and turns her friends against her. They organise events without letting her know. They start rumours about Angie. At first, she is confused. She hesitates to reach out. Then she feels terribly alone and isolated. She starts to spend more time in her bedroom on her devices. Her asthma returns, and she lies awake for hours at night. Six weeks later the doctor says she is depressed and prescribes antidepressant medication.

Paul worked for 25 years at a company. A downturn in the economy caused the business to fold. At 50, he finds himself without a job. At first, it is a terrible shock. Bravely he sets about looking for job. After dozens of applications, he does not get a single interview. Embarrassed, he starts to lie to his family and spends more time at the pub in the evenings. He drifts away from his family and friends. He stops exercising, gets terrible indigestion, and starts to put on weight. Six months later, he has a heart attack. It is a long road back…

And yet some people can go through far worse adversity: earthquakes, war, loss of a limb—and they Bounce. They make sense of the situation. They find ways to focus on the next step. They stay connected to those they love. They take care of themselves and maintain a sense of humour.

Resilience fails in predictable ways. Nature retained a set of self-protective behaviours through the evolution of reptiles, birds, and mammals because they work. We can understand the normal and natural rhythms of adversity, Bounce, and Growth.

My executive health clinic did extensive physical, emotional, and mental assessments for business leaders. These were capable people. Each year, out of 400 assessments, 20% presented with symptoms of depression. Of this group, only 10% understood and brought insight to their situation.

For the rest (90%), it was a shock. They had slowly spiralled their way down into depression. Once they understood the situation, their relief was obvious. A simple explanation gave them hope. I was stunned by the impact of awareness. This was the beginning of the Resilience Institute.

I stopped prescribing antidepressants from that day.

Rapid Bounce is a call for intelligent awareness and prevention. You can learn this process. When you master it, you own your Bounce process.

Rhythm

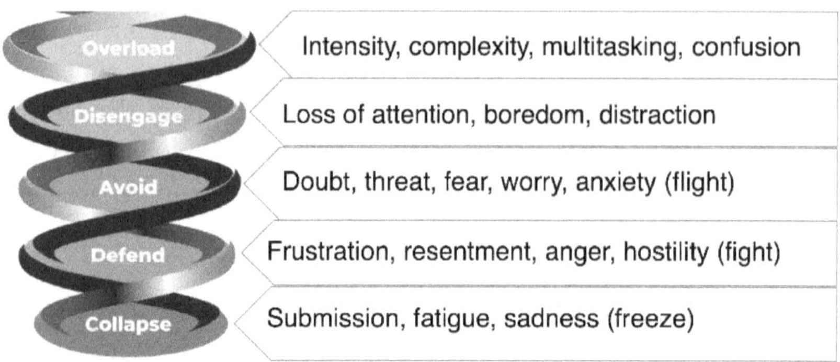

Figure 9: The stages of resilience failure or dissolution. This spiral has been simplified and aligned with Polyvagal Theory (explained below) since its previous form.

When secure, calm, and present, you are protected. When you lose this calm presence, resilience failure becomes a real risk. It can sneak up on you. Focus on what these stages mean to you. If you can identify and name it, you are on your way to rapid Bounce.

Stage 1: Overload (Cognitive Risk)

When your mind is calm and present to a task, you are absorbed, focused, and productive. As soon as your mind attaches to a second, third, or even fifth task, attention and productivity collapse. Multitasking is never productive. The world screams for our attention. We touch our phones 2,617 times per day on average. Switching attention is biologically costly. Adults switch every three minutes and teenagers every 19 seconds.[29]

We experience our days through a fog of overload, agitation, and mindless busyness. Attention leaps about—desire, act, and back again.

The executive attention network is in the prefrontal cortex (right behind your forehead). This part of the brain is perhaps 200,000 years old. It is expensive to run, guzzling oxygen and energy. ***Attention can operate only in short, focused bursts with periods of rest.*** Quality problem solving, learning and complex connections happen in these bursts. This is called the Task Positive Mode.

Most of us have exhausted this part of the brain by midmorning. Decision fatigue has been measured in multiple studies.[30] A famous study showed how judges granted most paroles in the first hours of the day. If you had your parole heard early, you had a 70% chance of going free. If it was the afternoon, fewer than 10% were granted.[31] We will learn more about this.

Mental Health and Overload

Overload starts the downward spiral and opens the door to suffering. True mental health disintegrates in the storm of information, deadlines, hopes, worries, frustrations, and regrets that define our lives.

Our mind has not yet evolved to cope with this information intensity. The digital age has allowed relentless, precise, and targeted attacks on our consciousness.

These are the first rumblings of distress. They are vague and difficult to name accurately. Many diagnose it as 'stress'. We include job confusion, overload, intensity, multitasking, and empathy fatigue as factors that contribute.

While this is not a mental illness, it is a state of reduced mental and intellectual function. Our capacity for attention, presence, renewal, decisiveness, and Flow is dramatically reduced. The experience of life is not satisfying.

Assailed by the chaos you tolerate and the mayhem of your agitated mind, the door to mental illness is wide open.

> **Drill 14: Define your experience of overload**
>
> How do you experience overload? Think back to times you have felt that your mind was running madly about with so many things to do. Can you remember how it felt? What were you thinking? Did it work out? Set an alarm to the time of day you are under the most pressure to wrap things up. When the alarm goes off, stop and take a note of what is going on. Check your body, name your emotions, watch the whirl of thoughts. When you can identify and name confusion, you can prevent suffering.

Stage 2: Disengage (Cognitive Failure)

Drawn to distraction by dopamine and failed by our attention network, the body saves energy by shutting the overloaded prefrontal cortex down. There is no warning and little awareness. One moment we are there, and the next we are gone. Neurobiologists enjoy reporting that 46% of the day, we are disengaged—body present and mind absent (presenteeism).

To be fair, this is the rest the brain needs for the next burst of attention. It is called the *default mode network*. The brain idles, rests, reflects, memorises, and renews. This is the engage-relax rhythm and the foundation of consciousness. ***Problems arise when the mind checks out without letting you know.*** Ever arrived in your driveway with no memory of the trip home from work? Ever find yourself in a room wondering why you wandered in there?

We have lost the luxury of rest and recovery rhythms. Frenetic switching of attention is so expensive that it threatens our maintenance functions. The body shuts attention down—like it stops a bleeding wound—to protect resources. Without warning, we find ourselves lost in daydreams or distracted by unhelpful fidgeting.

A meeting conclusion, leadership opportunities, and your own needs are lost. We make mistakes, let others down, and fail to achieve our goals.

When we disengage, our mature human responses are abandoned. The mind is no longer engaged in the situation. Conscious attention, perception, appraisal, evaluation, and proactive decision making are no longer available.

Primitive emotional and physical reactions take over. To date, we have found that this is one of the most useful learnings for leaders we work with. When we can identify this risk clearly, we feel empowered to solve it.

Mental Health and Disengage

When we disengage, we have attention failure or deficit. There is a normal rhythm to the switching between attention (task positive network) and relaxation (default mode networks). This rhythm is disrupted in schizophrenia, depression, bipolar disorder, anxiety, ADHD, autism, and post-traumatic distress.[32]

Hundreds of studies show this disrupted rhythm to be a clear neurobiological sign of mental illness. If Overload opens the door to suffering, Disengage allows you to walk right through. We need a rhythm between attention and relaxation. For each person this will be different. When this rhythm is disrupted, the mind fails.

For example, Pete was an active boy with a passion for swimming. In middle school, the swim coach left the school. Swimming was cancelled. To comfort him, his parents gave him a smartphone. With puberty came pimples and social awkwardness. Pete spent more time on his phone and less time being physically active (rhythm disruption).

Increasingly he spent his afternoons and evenings tapping, scrolling, and swiping. Like many young people today, his attention switched approximately every 18 seconds. To the shock of his parents, his teacher called a meeting. She described how agitated and unfocused he was. She suggested Pete should see a psychiatrist for ADHD. Within hours, Pete, age 14, was taking ADHD medication.

Rhythm

By 15, Pete's grades had improved. Teachers said he had become a good student. But "jacked" by the Ritalin, he started drinking alcohol to calm down (seeking rhythm). He discovered that he could sell his Ritalin to fund his drinking. He reinforced his learning that problems could be solved with chemicals.

Pete was lucky. His swim coach returned that year and begged him to join the team. With a mentor, structured training, and natural highs he stopped alcohol and found he no longer needed Ritalin. Coming home physically tired after two hours of training, deep sleep (normal rhythm) replaced tapping, scrolling, swiping, and medicating.

If persistent and disabling, Disengage is diagnosed as ADHD (Attention Deficit Hyperactivity Disorder) which has grown into a $24-billion USD amphetamine industry. Pete was fortunate in being able to reverse the downward spiral and get his life back on track. Today, 9.6 million Americans take ADHD medication.[33]

Remember, disrupted attention and relaxation rhythms are associated with the common causes of mental and emotional suffering. When you fail to take care of your engage-relax rhythm, you slip into the pit of despair.

Drill 15: Notice when you disengage

Take a moment to reflect on your typical day. When do you disengage? When have you been aware of it? When might you not be aware of it? What could you do to take the rest your brain needs before it disengages?

When you disengage randomly during daily living, your mind is no longer taking care of things. It is not even aware. Factors that may signal this risk include boredom, self-absorption, procrastination, forgetfulness, and attention loss.

If your mind is not engaged, you may ask what is running your life when you disengage?

I'll give you a clue: It is not your conscious mind.

Fortunately, evolution has retained a robust backup plan for exactly these situations. Through evolution, life coped with challenges rather well without the benefit of a conscious mind.

This is where Polyvagal Theory can help us.

Polyvagal Theory, Dissolution, and Mental Illness

As a second-year medical student, my job in anatomy was to dissect out the vagus nerve, the longest nerve in the body. Starting from two nuclei in the brainstem, it runs down with the carotid arteries (both sides), dives into the chest, heart, and lungs. Then, lower fibres drop through the diaphragm to the abdominal and pelvic organs. It took me six months to fully dissect the vagus nerve. We knew little about its functions.

The vagus nerve is the core of the parasympathetic system. It tells the brain what is going on inside the body. It activates the relaxation and digestion rhythms. In extreme situations, the old (dorsal) part triggers the freeze reaction.

The sympathetic nervous system runs down the spine and activates flight-and-fight reactions. Heart rate accelerates, blood pressure increases, and we fuel the muscles of avoidance and attack.

The Polyvagal Theory[34] by Stephen Porges was published in 2011. His most recent book, *Polyvagal Safety,* has just been released.[35] It explains the neurophysiology of our reactions and responses and has exploded into the mental health and counselling arena. (See Resources for the Polyvagal Institute website.) Here is a summary.

The sympathetic (adrenaline and mobilisation) and parasympathetic (relax and recover) nervous systems make up the autonomic (non-conscious) nervous system which is activated by neuroception. The body detects subtle cues from the environment that signal safety or risk. The nervous system is attuned to changes in visual, auditory, smell, taste, and touch signals. For example, dark shapes in the sky, growls, smell of blood, and angry faces will activate a threat reaction. The body is not safe. A reaction is triggered to protect the body.

The autonomic nervous system seeks homeostasis: a rhythm between activation and recovery. The sympathetic system accelerates us into action, and the vagus nerve calms and rejuvenates. Through the day, this rhythm paces us through challenges (heart rate up) balanced by relaxation and deep sleep (heart rate down). Your breath aligns with a gentle rhythm increasing heart rate slightly on inhalation and slowing it on exhalation (heart rate variability).

Polyvagal theory is simple and powerful. Beginning in early cells at the dawn of life, it plays out in the development and neural structures of humans 3.5 billion years later.

In overwhelming situations, the body draws on primitive or reptilian reactions. They are fast, crude, and robust. These reactions are hundreds of millions of years old. Humans have the ability to engage consciously with them. Let's see how these operate as resilience fails.

Stage 3: Avoid (Fear-Driven Flight Reactions)

Our conscious mind is a wonder of evolution—recent, powerful, and planet changing. When it fails, as in Disengage, our body feels exposed and at risk. It senses danger and knows that error is more likely.

This can progress to anxiety, fear, and panic. These are all layers of the flight reaction that happen below conscious awareness. Polyvagal theory calls this neuroception.

Sympathetic nerves use adrenaline (epinephrine) to shunt blood from brain, skin and gut to legs and buttocks in order to run. The snake and mouse flee for their lives. Humans jump back or leave the room. Under milder threats we may resort to lies and avoidance.

Deliberate, conscious thinking and our normal skills are not available when the emotion of fear takes over. We feel unsafe. We withdraw from action and engagement. Risks loom large.

Worry, anxiety, avoidance, hyper-vigilance, and fear symptoms activate. Fear makes us hesitant, uncertain, and anxious about consequences. Fear is the core of anxiety. For many, a pervasive low-grade anxious tension accompanies our waking hours. If we do not resolve this fear, it may progress into a generalised anxiety disorder.

Mental Health and Avoid

Anxiety is the most common mental illness. It is better described as an emotional disorder of excessive fear out of proportion to the threat. Worry is the related mental experience.

Anxiety symptoms (if persistent for more than two weeks, seek help):

- Excessive anxiety (fear) and worry
- Restlessness, irritability, and muscle tension
- Fatigue, difficulty concentrating, and sleep disturbance
- Panic attacks, phobias, and social anxiety
- Hyperventilation—rapid, shallow breathing

When prolonged, excessive fear leads to common distress symptoms. These might include digestive issues, muscle tension, chest pain and skin disorders. This is due to the shunting of blood from digestion and skin to muscles of flight.

Fear is a normal and sensible reaction to danger that helps us get out of harm's way. Usually, once safe, we relax and restore calm. Anxiety occurs when we fail to secure the relaxation response. In the relentless stimulation of modern life, the sympathetic reaction continues to flood our physiology. The vagal rest-and-digest rhythm fails to activate.

Anxiety becomes a perpetual state.

> **Drill 16: Catch your flight reactions**
>
> Where do you experience fear-based avoidance? What does it feel like? How might it look to those close to you? This is a pivot point in life. Once you can recognise and name it, you can stop the slide downwards.

Stage 4: Defend (Anger-Driven Fight Reactions)

If flight is not possible, the body selects the Defend or Attack reaction. The snake strikes and the mouse bites. We strike, scratch, bite, and shout. This is the sympathetic system activating anger.

We sense that our rights—or someone else's—have been violated. The organism focuses on a threat to blame and attack. Anger distorts our thinking in a very different way from fear. It focuses on a target to attack and fails to assess risk. Shouting, fighting, and rage may follow.

The sympathetic system activates adrenaline; blood shunts to the muscles of the shoulder (hitting, throwing), hands (grabbing, scratching), jaw (biting), and vocal cords (shouting). The prudent inner voice of caution and consequence fails.

Noradrenaline (norepinephrine) in the brain drives impatient, frustrated, quick, and impulsive reactions. We do or say things we regret. Others may perceive this as bullying. Check for the following factors: irritability, being overly critical, resentment, hostility, and direct anger.

Anger is the most dangerous emotion. Impulsive outbursts destroy trust in relationships. Anger may fester in a pervasive frustration, resentment, and desire for revenge. Hostility also is dangerous to health. It is correlated with depressed immune responses, inflammation, irregular heart rhythms and increased heart attack rates.

Driven by anger, we destroy our life—and the lives of others—one interaction at a time.

Mental Health and Defend

Anger reactions are labelled as conduct disorders. Unrestrained anger causes as much suffering as any mental illness. Consider the cost of shootings, street violence, speeding vehicles, bullying, domestic abuse, and terrorism, all driven by Defend (fight) reactions.

If our medical diagnostics label unresolved flight and fear as anxiety disorders and we label unresolved sadness as depression, surely, we might consider unresolved fight-and-anger states also to be a disorder. The suffering caused by anger is enormous—both to the person with anger and the people they interact with.

Given the simmering frustration and rage that define our times, perhaps labelling it more clearly might encourage restraint.

Drill 17: Catch your fight reactions

Where do you experience anger-driven reactions? What triggers activate frustration, anger, rage, and resentment in you? What does this feel like? What are the consequences? How does it look and feel to others?

Stage 5: Collapse (Fatigue and Sadness Freeze Reactions)

In an overwhelming situation, it may not be possible to run away or fight back. Sometimes the best alternative to preserve life is to play dead. This is the freeze reaction. Activated by old parts (dorsal nucleus) of the vagus nerve, blood pressure and pulse drop, bowels and bladder void, and the body 'plays dead'.

Rhythm

The snake rolls over, immobile. The mouse collapses in the jaws of a cat. Perhaps we leave the "dead" snake alone. Maybe the cat drops the mouse as the hunt is complete. Snake and mouse may survive another day. Neither snake nor mouse consciously makes the decision. The reaction is coded deeply into physiology.

Humans also freeze in overwhelming situations. In severe injury, we might faint. In battle, we can collapse, voiding bowels and bladder, just like a snake. In the face of violence such as rape or child abuse, freezing may be a sensible reaction. There is no point in attempting escape or resistance if we are overpowered. The ancient brain and body do what they can to preserve life.

In less severe situations, we may burst into tears, collapse, retreat to our bed or car. Mentally and emotionally, we withdraw inwards. Human freeze reactions deprive the brain of blood flow. And it is a dangerous reaction despite the life-saving potential. Afterwards it is hard to make sense of the reaction. The dissonance may be part of post-traumatic stress disorder. Understanding that the body was just doing the smartest thing under the circumstance can assist recovery.[36]

When we withdraw, we pull back to protect ourselves. We create distance between ourselves and others. Our energy drops. Watch for the following indicators: self-doubt, apathy, loneliness, anhedonia (loss of joy), and sadness.

When we withdraw, we lose confidence and reduce effort. We can spend long periods alone and retreat from work, friends, family, and enjoyable activities. We may feel tired, sad, lonely, guilt, shame, and bereft of hope. Our tendency is to collapse and submit. We perceive the threat(s) as overwhelming. Flight and fight are no longer options.

Mental Health and Collapse

If we cannot resolve the withdrawal, fatigue, and submission associated with the freeze reaction, it can progress to sadness and depression, now the second-most-common mental illness.

Depression takes various forms. It has complex causes involving genes (inheritance), early life distress, and illness. We cannot do much about what has happened in the past, other than strive to forgive, learn any practical lessons from it, and recognise the risk. Sometimes in gaining clarity about our own experiences, we can help others at risk become more aware of how resilience might fail. When it does, this model provides hope.

Symptoms of depression include:

- Loss of joy (anhedonia), tears, hopelessness
- Decreased energy, persistent sadness and low mood
- Social withdrawal or loss of concentration
- Sleep disorder (usually waking early and unable to get back to sleep)
- Feeling unmotivated to work, exercise, or even get out of bed
- Change of appetite and / or weight
- Loss of concentration, confusion, overwhelm, indecisiveness
- Thoughts of self-harm.

If persistent for more than two weeks, or if you feel you are losing the will to live, or feel a strong urge to harm yourself or others, please seek professional help. I also encourage you to reach out to family, friends, neighbours, anyone who may be supportive in your local community. There are also many excellent online crisis centres where you can phone or text, in many cases anonymously. Please see Resources.

Drill 18: Catch your freeze reactions

Where do you immobilise in the face of adversity? What triggers activate withdrawal? How does it feel? What might others notice? How does this affect your relationships?

Rhythm

When flight, fight, and freeze reactions remain active over time, our physical, emotional, and mental integrity break down. In this view, those reactions are emotional and physiological disorders based on ancient biological mechanisms. The biological state of body and emotion lead to the mental patterns characteristic of these disorders.

The human mind can of course generate thoughts which may activate the emotions. If I worry about a potential risk, this will trigger a feeling of anxiety (fear). If I ruminate on an offensive comment, I can activate anger. If I keep focusing on a failure or loss, this will trigger sadness.

In humans, the sequence of suffering can be both bottom up and top down. Bottom up, the biological reaction erupts in the body, activating the emotional state, which triggers the related thinking. Top down, we generate a chain of thoughts, activating emotions which then trigger physical reactions.

Either way, when your resilience fails, you most likely will experience physical changes. The acute reactions of flight, fight, and freeze are rapid and potentially overwhelming. They take hold of your body before you have time to think. Afterwards, you can feel shocked by the power and intensity of your reaction.

With unresolved fear, anger, and sadness, over time we accumulate signs of distress. This has been referred to as chronic stress. We may feel it in sleep disturbance, gut or skin irritability, muscle tension, chest symptoms, or headaches. Your body is calling for attention and care. Bounce is urgent and critical.

Respect these symptoms and take care of yourself. Listen and respond with care and skill.

Many years back, while completing my MBA, I fell deeply into distress through some business challenges. The weather had been terrible, exercise collapsed, sleep was short and disturbed, and a relationship was ending.

Dr. Sven Hansen

Sitting still while a hairdresser worked on an itchy scalp felt like agony. My fists were clenched in my lap. My jaw was rigid. My stomach was like a plank, and for the first time, I sensed that I was breathing too fast and too high.

What a picture I must have been for the hairdresser! Somehow, I had to stop and be still in the chair. Pushing too hard, I had sunk down the resilience spiral believing that I was unbreakable. Great awakening. I have been more sensitive and respectful since.

Burnout is a poor label. Humans do not burn out. Yes, we suffer and sometimes our tank feels empty. Burnout is final and disabling. It is not a clinical or biological condition. When you feel depleted, it is better to call it distress.

Drill 19: Name and tame your symptoms of distress.

1. Feelings of nervousness, anxiety or worry

2. Trouble getting to sleep or restless sleep

3. Irritability, grumpiness, or angry outbursts

4. Lump in throat or difficulty swallowing

5. Rapid shallow breathing or shortness of breath

6. Irritable bowel, diarrhea, constipation, or gut pain

7. Headache, migraine, or eye strain

8. Muscle tension, sore neck, or tight shoulders

9. Wheezing, coughing, or tightness in chest

10. Pain in chest (left side), fast or irregular heartbeat.

Rhythm

Resilience failure can progress over long periods of time. We spiral down slowly over days or months—so slowly, we don't notice. This is why it is essential to recognise the signs and the stages. At times the associated distress leads to illness. Some examples:

A driven athlete trains through the off season. She pushes herself relentlessly into overtraining syndrome. She collapses at the start of the season and is put on antidepressants. Recovery takes three months.

Two young parents with jobs and children struggle 24x7 to keep up with relentless tasks, pressures, and complications. They feel like failures at parenting and at their professions.

A CEO compromises health and family as he wrestles a company through years of difficulty and conflict. Ignoring high blood pressure readings, he has a stroke at 48.

A social marketer works on a device, touching it 4,000 times per day—and night. Her sleep structure and timing collapse. She is diagnosed with burnout and told to take a month off from work. There is no such diagnosis in the DSM-5 (Diagnostic and Statistical Manual of Mental Disorders). It is a popular term to label what we have been discussing. In my view, burnout is a term we should use for candles, not for human beings.

We live in a world wrestling with resilience failure. It has been normalized. Millions leave doctors' offices with diagnoses of ADHD, social anxiety, PTSD, autism, generalised anxiety, sleep disorder, inflammatory disease, and depression. Mostly, we throw drugs at the problems.

Understanding how resilience fails can show you the way to Bounce. We over-diagnose and over-medicate. And we don't address the root causes. With this understanding, you can be an informed and resourceful agent in your own recovery. Step back with insight and these episodes become opportunities for "post-traumatic growth".

Finally, we have to confront the mental health of young people.[37] This is a testing time for teens and young adults. While many thrive, others are isolated and bewildered by the risks of solving the complex threats facing their future. There is evidence that mobile devices, excessive use of social media or video games, and sleep disturbances cause mental illness.

Some young people have been over-protected from physical, emotional and mental adversity. For example, play and exploration is limited by safety concerns. Conflict is avoided in education. Uncomfortable concepts and literature are removed from debate. We have removed many challenges that stimulate growth. Avoidance, rather than engagement with adversity, fails to stimulate post-traumatic growth as articulated by Haidt and Lukianof in *Coddling of the American Mind*.[38]

We must be deliberate in acknowledging resilience failure. Perhaps with this knowledge, we can cultivate a skilled growth mindset in adversity.

In conclusion, going down the spiral is unsafe. Life is not secure. Our biological reactions become ever more desperate as the pressure on our survival increases. Yet these are normal processes that can be understood. We know that seeing these stages of resilience failure can be lifesaving. Resilience helps people in trouble—and those who love them—make sense of a scary experience. It also provides a pathway to Bounce forward fast.

> **Drill 20: Define each stage of resilience failure for yourself**
>
> Take some time to describe in your own experience and words what each stage is like for you. If you can notice it, you are ready to Bounce forward fast.

Rhythm

Summary of Resilience Failure

Stages	Signals, signs, and symptoms
Overload	Crazy busy, multitasking, switching tasks madly, head feels full and muddled
Disengage	Staring into space, others call me out, forget names of people introduced or why I am in this room, losing track of tasks or items
Avoid	Uncertainty, self-doubt, anxiety, fear, worry, procrastination…
Defend	Frustrated, impatient, angry, resentful, ruminating on bad events…
Collapse	Loss of energy, "giving up", retreating, isolating, sadness, loss of hope…

Next up is how to Bounce forward fast.

Bounce Forward Fast

The purpose of this chapter is to show you how to Bounce forward fast and Grow in adversity. Bounce ranks as the third most important factor for optimal resilience in our 2022 research.

Most people use the term "Bounce Back". This is impossible in living tissue. Adversity creates challenge and adaptation. You learn and Grow. You cannot go backwards. An athlete trains under unpleasant pressure. Tissue damage stimulates an increase in power, speed, endurance, and attention.

We Bounce forward. We learn, adapt, and improve.

In this chapter, you will learn skills and confidence to Bounce forward fast. You will learn to Bounce at the earliest suggestion of resilience failure. There are limitless, creative ways to get this done. You can be a master of Bounce. You will welcome adversity as a necessary rhythm for your development.

Bounce is the best-known aspect of resilience. Seventy years of research demonstrates the importance of Bounce. All living beings confront illness, injury, adversity, loss, or disaster. Life has evolved to Bounce. Recovery, adaptation, and improvement is the natural process. Humans are no different.

Respect this natural Bounce. It is a powerful force. It has made us a formidable species.

A successful lawyer came in as a patient early in my career. He had resigned from his firm that day and was facing both work and marriage difficulty. Assessment revealed he was depressed. Over six months of overwork and self-neglect, he became truly disabled. The key symptoms were early morning waking, confusion, withdrawal, and loss of joy (anhedonia). Once he understood what had happened, he asked how he could recover without antidepressants. It was a novel challenge to address. Most sought antidepressants.

Rhythm

I recommended exercise every second day, sleep discipline, and simple reframing of negative thoughts. Armed with insight and skills, he went straight back to work to withdraw his resignation. He recovered within six weeks. This was a turning point for me as much as for him. He remained a high-performing partner in the firm for another 25 years.

Traditional medical care often follows a script: "You have been disabled by a disease called depression. The chemicals in your brain are imbalanced. This requires medication. I want you to take these powerful new antidepressants and come back to see me in two weeks. Take six weeks off work."

The patient is labelled and removed from the solution. They end up isolated and distressed at home. They lose their connection with colleagues and satisfying work. This is a common story that seldom has a happy outcome.

The future could be: "This is what happened, and this is how you are part of it. It is normal. You can direct your own recovery".

Here are three actions you can take immediately. The more committed you are to your Bounce practice, the faster your recovery. Don't make important life decisions now. Stay engaged and be deliberate in executing your recovery plan. This works.

If you have been down the spiral, you already are intrinsically motivated to master Bounce. Resilience failure leads to suffering: mental, emotional, and physical. Bounce is a natural, self-directed discipline to counter and relieve suffering so you can Bounce upward into a calm, engaged, and connected state.

Bounce offers you a simple, evidence-based method to get out of trouble. Just as there is a logic to how resilience fails, so there is logic and sequence to Bounce forward fast.

Figure 10: The Bounce stages and process

We will work from the bottom of the spiral upwards. You don't always hit rock bottom. It is good to have a plan in mind. With practice, you will learn how to Bounce out of the smallest hint of overload or disengage. This Bounce can be instantaneous. When you sink lower, you must be patient and determined in your efforts.

Bounce is reinforced by daily practice. When we get good sleep, maintain fitness, relax, and eat well (basic lifestyle rhythm) we have a strong buffer of vitality and altitude that counters adversity. Rebuilding this daily practice as you Bounce is essential.

Bounce in Collapse and Freeze

In a Freeze reaction, the old vagus nerve drives collapse under threat. It is a normal reaction to take care of yourself in a major threat. Submission is better than being destroyed. Unresolved Freeze reactions may consolidate to fatigue and depression.

First, name it clearly and accept it. You have collapsed and withdrawn. It is time to reconnect. Find a safe and trusting relationship to get support. Use an expert you respect to define and understand what happened. An objective understanding of your experience is the beginning of recovery.

Take the time you need to rest and recover. Know that recovery time will bring you back stronger. A few days away from work, close to nature with adequate sleep is generally enough.

Reach out to positive people. This reconnection is the key reframe required when we feel depressed and isolated. Explain the experience as a learning. Use positive and realistic terms. Engage in activities that you enjoy. This might be reading, walking, exercise, nature, time with friends or sport.

Small challenges that stimulate the sympathetic system such as a brisk walk will re-energise you. Sunshine reactivates the vagal tone. Slow breathing (see below), cold water, gargling, laughing, and singing help.

In a more severe case, you may feel prolonged sadness, confusion, fatigue, and pessimism. Have the courage and humility to reach out to a qualified person. Depression is diagnosed when symptoms persist for two weeks or more (see resilience failure). Professional advice is important. Explore your options carefully. Medication is not always the first step. Seek alternative opinions, as you must be engaged in your treatment plan.

Sleep, quiet environments, gentle activity, journaling, massage, healthy eating, yoga, and nature are proven to be effective. Seek out an expert to guide you in reframing your thoughts, self-compassion, and building positive emotions. Cognitive behaviour therapy (CBT) is well proven.

Drill 21: Get help, understand, and describe fully what is going on

In Freeze/Collapse reactions, we can lose the desire to care for ourselves. You are unlikely to be able to help others if you cannot help yourself. Be kind to yourself. Taking a full weekend off with no phones or devices is my preferred practice. Reconnect with activities and people that give you joy. Reignite your sources of joy, love, gratitude, and awe. Nature nurtures and can be a good friend.

Drill 22: Self compassion in distress

Sit quietly in a comfortable upright position. Close your eyes, relax your face, and exhale completely. Gently inhale, appreciating the oxygen activating your cells. Exhale and let any bad feelings escape and dissolve. Focus attention on your heart. As you inhale, concentrate on feeling caring and kind to yourself. Feel the softening in your chest and heart area. Exhale and relax. Repeat the cycle for five minutes.

You often feel cut off from others. You may be embarrassed. Perhaps you let someone down and feel judged. We desperately want connection but reaching out is difficult. It is tempting to reach for a social media platform to connect. Don't. It may take you deeper into misery.

To activate the new and myelinated part of the vagus nerve, face-to-face contact is helpful. Find someone who makes you feel good. Eye contact, touch, upper face movement (smiley and kind eyes), a gentle voice, or uplifting music bring us back to ourselves.

Exhale long, slow, and easy. Breathe in for four seconds and out for six. Listen to music, nature sounds, or voices that make you feel good. Relax your face—especially the mouth, tongue, and jaw. Smiling and laughing are genuinely therapeutic.

When we feel down, the impulse is to distance ourselves from others. The critical reframe is to Connect. Come out of your cave / cocoon / shell. Open your shoulders, lift your chin, and raise your eyes. Move towards others and back into engagement with life. Yes, it is hard. Everything you feel says you want to go deeper into the cave and hide. But walk out and reconnect anyway.

Choose your support network with care. Don't underestimate the value of pets—particularly dogs. For most of our evolution, dogs have been close friends. We know they activate our connection systems strongly and play an important role in healing.

Rhythm

Our family dog, a golden retriever, had the wise and compassionate eyes of a priest. Benny was totally dialled in to our moods. If one of us was down, he would wander over, place his head on our lap and look straight into our eyes. His amazing power to connect was a huge source of love, comfort, and strength.

Drill 23: Connect with nature and consider (wisely) a pet

Being close to nature has a powerful healing effect on body, heart and mind. Ideally, 20 minutes per day or 150 minutes of time in nature secures the positive effects. Seek out what feels best for you—forest, ocean, rivers, plains, birds or animals. Even a plant in your home or a view of a tree has benefits. It is well known that a pet can assist healing. Be sensible about the responsibility of caring for a pet. Perhaps take care of a friend's dog.

Expect rapid recovery. Use every available hand and foot hold. Move upwards. Well-structured lifestyle discipline is recommended. It is hard to motivate oneself consistently, so find a coach to help you exercise, eat well, practice relaxation, and find positivity in your daily activities. I also recommend *Lost Connections* by Johan Hari.[39] This is a carefully researched and rich resource for understanding suffering and how to reconnect with life and what matters.

Drill 24: Practice compassion for those suffering

Take note when those you love or work with withdraw. They may become quiet, avoid contact, or isolate themselves. Reach out to them in person. Ask how they are doing and show your concern. The faster you can connect with someone withdrawing, the quicker they will Bounce. It is a key to good leadership, friendship, and parenting. Practicing compassion is good for both parties. It is also the quickest way to feel good. Be good by doing good.

Bounce in Defend and Fight

In Fight, we have activated the sympathetic system with anger. The impulse is to attack. This is a dangerous state both for your health and for those you care about.

In anger, you feel distressed. You notice tension in your face, neck, and shoulders. Your breathing and heart rate are accelerated. You may be flushed and agitated. You might desire revenge.

Pay attention because this is one of the most important sentences in this book and guidelines for your life: ***Never act out of this state of anger.***

Pause and name the feeling of anger and the urge to attack.

To tame fight and anger, you must slow things down. Remove yourself from the trigger. Take time to let your body settle. Use Tactical Calm (next chapter) to slow your breathing, lower your heart rate, and drop your blood pressure. If you feel rage, it may be worth heading outside and exercising. Constructive activity directs and releases the energy in more helpful ways. Walk, run, dance, swim (my favourite), or stretch.

Rhythm

The once-popular practice of venting anger is no longer considered useful. Hitting a pillow or shouting at the moon simply strengthens anger. The trick is to soften and dissolve your anger.

The next step is to flex your perspective on the situation. An angry mind has distorted tunnel vision. What you see is not the full situation. Your mind will ruminate (chew the cud) over and over as it replays the biased perspective. This blocks clear perception and thinking.

The reframe is to generate respect and understanding for the target of your anger. Explore what else might be going on for them. Did the perpetrator that you feel such anger and resentment towards really intend to hurt you? Could you be a contributor in any way to the conflict?

As you step back from focused anger, work at seeing different perspectives. Remember the good parts of your life, the people you love, and the good elements of someone who may have upset you. See the bigger picture. Know that you are part of a community. We crave connection and acceptance.

Generate a more constructive story. Can you give them the benefit of doubt? Could there have even been a positive intention? If not, was their behaviour part of a habitual pattern they do with other people too (thus it was not personal)? Can you forgive?

Once again, finding a sense of kindness toward yourself can be very helpful. Remember that your anger is doing you damage. It is in your interest to move quickly away from anger. Let the sympathetic, anger-driven reaction melt into connection and increased vagal tone. Be the bigger person.

Drill 25: Dealing with anger

Anger can be explosive, so pick your battles. Preventing an outburst of anger can save a team or a family. If successful, you improve outcomes for all those involved. Be discrete and direct. For example: *I imagine you might be upset about that.* Help the person accept and name their anger. Remind them that anger drives bad decisions. Help them see different perspectives. For example: *They have been a good client for many years. We all mess up sometimes. Let's win the war not the battle.*

Bounce in Avoid and Flight

In Flight, the sympathetic system is activated with fear. The impulse is to escape or avoid a threat. Fear increases heart and breath rate. Blood rushes downwards, and we may feel pressure to avoid, evade, escape, or even lie. As in anger, fear interferes with our thinking. This time, we will find worry loops invading our minds.

As with Freeze and Fight, Flight is a normal response to a significant challenge, threat, or disruption. The body has chosen to avoid confrontation by escaping.

In a panic attack or phobia, the reaction is overwhelming. We need time to tame it before we can name it. Try to anticipate these situations and be well prepared. If you are determined to visit the spider display with a spider phobia, breathe slowly. Keep repeating: *The spiders are in special cages. I am totally safe and can always leave.* You are naming, taming, and reframing in advance.

A clear, objective description of your state is the turning point. The reframe is to move toward safety and recovery as fast as possible. There are times when a safe distance is an excellent idea—even if you feel foolish afterwards.

Rhythm

Unresolved fear can become anxiety which is usually associated with worry. This is the most common cause of suffering today. It sneaks up on us. Anxiety and worry take over our emotional and mental experience.

I have found it helpful to run a daily preventive check. I scan the day for moments of anxiety or worry. Time pressure and upsetting others are common themes. I remind myself that I am fine (relaxed and safe) and resolve to stay present in the moment.

In polyvagal theory, this is a critical transition point. Fear and anxiety are there to propel us back to safety and connection. The first step in this direction is to *ritualise your daily relaxation practice.* This might be breathing, meditation, prayer, massage, or time with loved ones. We devote the next chapter to this.

In the meantime, start to think about how you might activate your movement to safety at each nudge of anxiety or worry.

Drill 26: Dissolving anxiety symptoms

1. Deliberate, slow diaphragmatic breathing practice

2. Facilitated relaxation (massage, yoga, tai chi)

3. Talk things through with loved ones or a counsellor

4. Prayer on the fly or a one-minute meditation

5. Gentle aerobic exercises, stretching, and yoga

6. Stop alcohol, junk food, and stimulants for two weeks

7. Spend time in nature and close to water when you can.

At first, this does not feel natural. It brings up guilt and frustration. It is frustrating and boring. Persist because it delivers surprising benefits. The parasympathetic system will kick in, and you feel the comfort of safety. The more expert you become at activating the relaxation response, the simpler this powerful Bounce drill becomes. You have powered up your parasympathetic system (vagal tone).

Bounce in Disengaged

We cannot stay focused effectively for long periods. Many of us can be disengaged for 50% of the day. Mastering Bounce if we have disengaged takes insight and skill.

The brain phases naturally from attention to disengaged as a default mode that allows the brain to idle. Key elements of memory, reflection, learning, and rest are integrated. The correct phasing of this on-off rhythm in the brain is essential for optimal function and mental health. We discussed how in schizophrenia, depression, and attention disorders this rhythm is disrupted.

Today we have little idle time. When we might have taken a nap or watched the flowers bloom, now we snatch up a phone and desperately prod away at multiple urgent and unimportant disturbances. Every break in the day is filled with digital dopamine hits. The natural pauses for the default mode have been removed. Thus, the brain runs flat out until it fails. We disengage in full flight with no warning or awareness.

Our challenge is to recognise this rhythm. How long can you stay focused? How much rest do you need, and when, to keep refocusing through the day?

Drill 27: Periodise your day

Work out how long an optimal focus period is for you—between 3 and 20 minutes. Then determine how much time you need in default mode to rejuvenate attention. Seek a rhythm to give your best to a task and take the break consciously so that your brain can idle, consolidate, and refuel.

Finally, work out how to periodise or "chunk" your day in a sustainable way. To improve productivity, create protected space around your key tasks. Put the phone somewhere else and turnoff all your communication platforms other than the one you are working on, and all notifications. If you are disturbed by a text or notification, it can take 30 minutes to get back to the same level of productivity. Start a conversation at home or at the office about how you can support each other to be productive.

I work best in ten-minute bursts before I need a stretch or breathing break. Ideally, every half hour I get up and do something different for 2 to 5 minutes. Remember that if you switch across five tasks (e-mail, message, Facebook, spreadsheet, weather), you lose 75% of your mental energy during that period.

The symptoms of sleep deprivation are the same as attention disorders. The complex rhythms of sleep are an essential part of restoring the brain and preparing it for the next day. We will tackle sleep in Part 3 but for now, start to think about how you can build in more breaks between bursts of single-minded focus, and how you can get more sleep.

> **Drill 28: Effective rejuvenation between focus bursts**
>
> Take three slow diaphragmatic breaths.
>
> Do one long, quiet nasal exhalation followed by a pause (2 seconds).
>
> Stretch, balance, or enjoy a brief walk.
>
> Powernap for 10 minutes.
>
> Go out in nature and be in sunlight for 20 minutes.
>
> Use a standing desk to lift your productivity.
>
> Keep protein snacks (nuts, chicken), healthy-fat snacks (nuts, avocado) and coffee/tea/lemon water handy.
>
> Sit upright and breathe (6 sec out, 4 sec in) for one minute every hour.

Discipline in Overload

We have a limited amount of time to be calm and focused. We can Bounce rapidly if we use our attention with respect and skill. Our busy world is likely to accelerate further. Chunk up your tasks into single bursts of attention. Once you have a plan for the day, select the key task for this moment and give it 100% of your attention. Work in short bursts and take regular, short breaks. Once you have hit a milestone, take a decent break. Celebrate your progress and recharge for the next task.

Be ruthless in selecting what is important. We are under assault. Everybody wants a bit of our attention and the skill with which advertising is getting our attention is alarming. Many people are checking multiple platforms dozens of times per day.

If you want to succeed in your relationships, your work, your study, and your creativity, be very tough about protecting yourself from distractions.

A wonderful habit is to allocate 90 minutes during the first three hours of your day to do the really important stuff. Mental resources are sharpest in the morning for most people. For some, it may be later in the day. This is your Flow time—a core skill we address in the last chapter.

Select 1-3 tasks that can really move you forward, and schedule them into your morning before life interrupts. Shut down all distractions. Educate those you work or live with that this is your Flow time. The feeling of accomplishment that follows establishment of this power habit is priceless.

Drill 29: Engage in Flow

Focus on one task at a time.

Delete what is not important.

Delegate everything you possibly can.

Take frequent micro-breaks during intense work.

Sharpen your priority list to no more than two issues.

Tackle your most important tasks during your Flow time.

Base camp is to be calm, alert, engaged, and present to the experience unfolding around you. Sounds easy but it is actually very hard. The muscles required to stay here are breath control, contentment, and attention. Let's see how good you are.

Drill 30: Open presence

Take five minutes to explore this.

> Just sit and see if you can let yourself be completely calm.

> Be there with your muscles relaxed, your face soft, and your breathing slow and low.

> Explore being content. Accept yourself and the moment fully.

> Bring your attention to be fully focused and present to the moment.

> Open your senses of smell, hearing, sight, taste, and touch, one at a time.

> You are learning the state of open presence.

So obvious, but how often do you take a moment to rest and be centred in this state? Notice the impulse to do something: check this, read that, must run, go do …. Watch your thoughts swirl, then seek solutions. We grasp at how the past should have been or how the future should be. This moment—the only moment we ever live in—is lost as we spiral off into busyness, agitation, or boredom. Our lives are comprised of a series of present moments. Getting better at living in them will make all the difference for you.

Once you understand the spiral, its stages, and the steps to prevent a slide, you can live your life with much more confidence and awareness. Further, you can manage periods of extreme challenge with intelligence. You will understand the risks and the signals prior to error. In the short run, you can manage the strain. Remember to plan a proper restorative break once you have completed the challenge.

Rhythm

Summary of Bounce

Stages	Bounce practice
Overload	Single task focus, short bursts, schedule Flow time…
Disengage	Get up and stretch between bursts, powernap, walk about, and connect…
Avoid/Flight	Relax, be in the moment, exhale, buddy up on a challenge…
Defend/Fight	Slow down, take a wide view, respect and explore others' points of view…
Collapse/Freeze	Seek out a high-trust connection, set small goals, move, walk, get in nature…

Now that you understand the practical steps to Bounce in adversity, we will address the fundamental skill of relaxation or Tactical Calm.

Tactical Calm

The purpose of this chapter is to understand how to secure a state of calm, control, and connection quickly and effectively. Our research places relaxation as the fourth most important factor for optimal resilience.

Rest (biological rejuvenation) is the natural process of recovery and rebuilding that follows effort. We need quality rest to improve performance and life. In general, we are poor at this. When we rest, our heart slows, blood pressure drops, breathing slows, the body repairs, and cells rebuild. We feel calm and relaxed with a sense of relief, satisfaction, and pleasure. The mind slows down. Sleep and digestion improve.

In the chapter on how resilience fails, we described how the sympathetic and parasympathetic systems play out under threat. Here we explore the beneficial calm, control, and connect components of the vagus nerve.

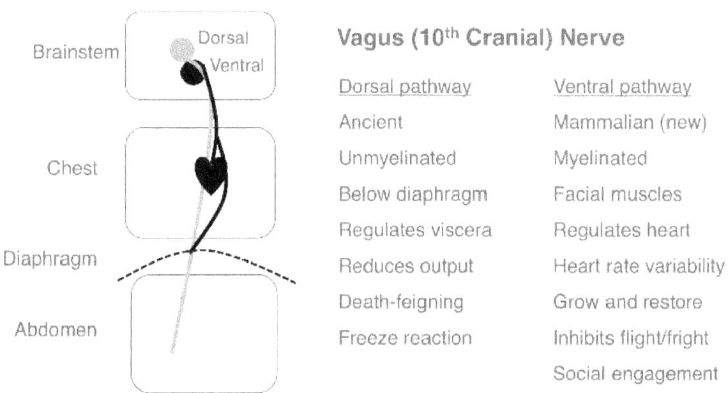

Figure 11: Simplified diagram showing the vagus nerve components

Polyvagal Theory postulates two components of the vagus nerve or tenth cranial nerve. The old rest, digest, and freeze elements we have discussed. The new myelinated fibres come from the ventral nucleus. These regulate facial muscles controlling expression, hearing, and voice as well as the heart. When active, health and restoration are optimized, and the social engagement system enables safety, calm and social interaction. The vagus fibres run primarily from body to brain (bottom up). About twenty percent run from brain to body (top down).

When the ventral vagal pathway activates, it is first a biological brake that slows the heart and restores coherent heart rate variability. We calm down, restore, and rejuvenate. Health improves and inflammation reduces.

Second, the ventral fibres through their connection with facial muscles, hearing, and voice activate our social engagement system. This is called the heart-face connection.

Social engagement means that we feel safe to trust and connect with others. Eye contact increases, our voice becomes prosodic (rhythmic like a lullaby), and hearing is attuned to higher-frequency tones. These changes are the foundation of empathy, positive emotion, trust, and play.

The excellent news is that we can train the vagus nerve. The newer parts will myelinate if we practice relaxation and calm responses to challenge. Myelin is a fatty insulator that helps the nerve conduct the calming and signals faster. Imagine your favourite athlete, yogi, emergency worker, or soldier with a well-myelinated vagus nerve. That is how they stay calm and focused in adversity.

With a trained vagus nerve, the sympathetic system is a smooth accelerator. Our body, heart, and mind gear up to tackle a challenge. We can motivate ourselves with emotion, and then focus on the challenge. This acceleration system drives our performance into Flow. Our heart accelerates, blood pressure increases, breathing is faster, and muscles power up.

Pressure is intense in a grand slam tennis final. Millions of people watching on TV, huge stadium, money at stake, and seriously competitive pressure. It is physically, emotionally, and mentally demanding. The great players work hard at staying calm in order to support flow.

They control their breathing, relax muscles and face, and stay in the moment. At times they press into peak performance—but not too much.

We all have seen how tennis players can slip into the fight reaction, smash their rackets, or swear. If they do so, they almost always lose and may face a severe fine.

If we accelerate too fast, we lose control and crash. We press ourselves into Flight, Fight, and/or Freeze. The ventral vagus nerve can be trained.

Drill 31: Vagal brake options

Focus on long, slow exhalations through the nose.

Practice measured diaphragmatic breath (see below).

Focus your attention on a loved one (oxytocin effect).

Relax your face and neck and let yourself smile.

Massage your neck or abdomen.

Schedule deep-tissue massage into your week.

Splash cold water on your face.

Swim, especially underwater.

Listen to the right music (prosodic rhythms).

Do yoga and/or meditation.

Laugh, gargle, or go out in the sunlight

Once the vagus nerve is trained and myelinated, new options emerge.

Rhythm

Your recovery from training or testing days is much faster. The heart slows, muscles relax, nutrition is better, immunity improves, and a good sleep is much more likely. Rapid recovery from pressure is the foundation of Bounce and Flow facilitated by an activated vagal nerve.

Human collaboration requires a state of relaxation, safety and trust. The ventral vagal pathway holds us in a state of safety and trust which enables constructive interaction, communication, and problem solving.

Intimacy requires the ventral pathway to work with the dorsal pathway to maintain a calm and responsive state with physical contact. In cases of abuse or some forms of autism, feeling comfortable and safe with close physical contact is challenging. Clinicians are increasingly working with vagal training techniques to help patients build a sense of safety in physical contact.[40]

Another key element is play. Play is vital to develop and prepare for life. Play requires the ventral vagal parasympathetic pathways to work alongside the sympathetic system. The sympathetic system allows us to approach (imagine two kittens posturing at the start of play), chase, run away, and wrestle. The energetic activity of play is essential for the development of strength, speed, and coordination.

For play to be safe and effective, the ventral vagal pathways must be active. Even when kittens play, they naturally engage in strong eye contact, they exhibit expressive eyes and emit squeals of delight and laughter. Young mammals, including our children, are learning to understand others, anticipate reactions, show empathy and restrain excess fight-and-flight reactions. Adults as well as children need more play today.

Under extreme performance pressure, the sympathetic system needs to be strongly activated along with the ventral vagus. This is obvious in the relaxed intensity of elite performance. These resources can be activated, trained, and applied creatively to help us play and perform better in life.

Dr. Sven Hansen

The autonomic nervous system is an intervening variable in the range of functional states from Freeze and Fight up to play and performance as shown below. By mastering the calm and connect system of the new vagal pathways, we can move from reactive to responsive solutions to life. We use the term *Tactical Calm* to represent this practical skill to respond successfully to challenge.

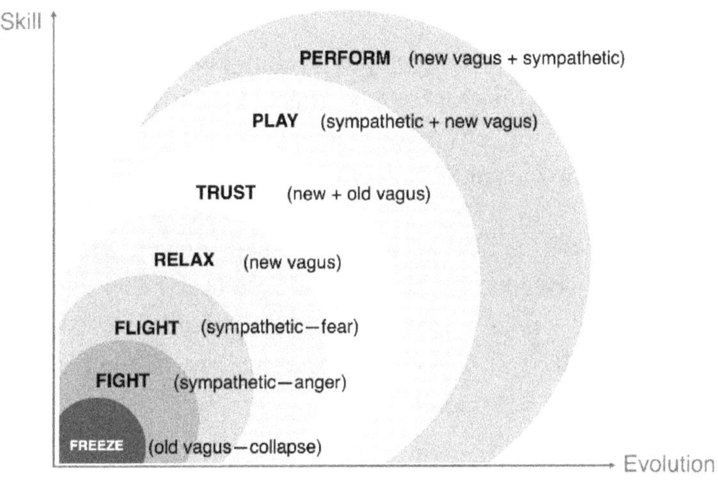

Figure 12: Autonomic nervous system enabling functional states

When we apply Tactical Calm, we move rapidly from distressed to a relaxed and effective state. This calming effect accelerates Bounce and is the base of optimal performance—or Flow. An effective solution is a foundation for your resilience.

When an organism confronts a threat, the metabolism increases to drive rapid evasive or aggressive action. Most threats in evolution are short-lived. Natural relaxation and recovery follow within seconds.

According to The American Institute of Stress:

Rhythm

- About 33 percent of people report feeling extreme stress;
- 77 percent of people experience stress that affects their physical health; and
- 73 percent of people have stress that impacts their mental health.[41]

It is clear that many of us feel distressed in our hyperactive and over-stimulated world. Threats—real and imagined—assail us continuously. Feeling safe, relaxed and trusting is rare. For many, relaxation can generate further guilt and anxiety.

Tactical Calm is a simple, practical adjustment to shift yourself toward an effective response. The more regularly you execute your practice, the more effective you become. You establish a strong base camp at Secure on the spiral.

I recently coached a young basketball player. He was highly motivated and very good for his age. During a trial, he was unable to sink the shots that he would normally make easily. Under selection pressure, he found himself over thinking, hesitating, and feeling anxious. His ability to shoot in Flow disintegrated.

He became anxious and upset. It was a miserable trial for him and put his season at risk. Pressure poured down from coach, colleagues, and parents.

I taught him how to apply Tactical Calm. By helping him define and drill a simple practice that he could use at key points in the next trial, he had an excellent outcome. In his father's words:

The difference was remarkable. He took three things into the Saturday trials:

1. Breathe for four seconds in and six seconds out.
2. Breathe out when you shoot, and don't hesitate.
3. Celebrate every shot—successful or not.

He came out very happy with his performance. "The change from the previous week was incredible."

Under pressure, we are compromised by too much sympathetic activity. Remember this distress—heart going too fast, anxious, worried, and confused. The body becomes stiff, we cannot focus, and performance collapses. This can happen in sports, public speaking, exams, arguments, dates, or facing phobias like fear of heights, water, or closed spaces. Many give up their passions as a result.

With Tactical Calm, we learn to apply the brakes, relax the muscles, calm the emotions, and focus the mind.

Once you master Tactical Calm, you can master difficult challenges, reduce anxiety, and perform with confidence. This allows you to enjoy nearly everything life throws your way, with skill and pleasure.

Here is how to become expert at Tactical Calm. Complete this chart for three situations in your life where you could really use the benefits of Tactical Calm. These can be personal or professional.

Describe the specific situation	What happens when you get anxious?	What do you want to achieve?

If you can be calm and effective when others choke or panic, the future is yours. You will sleep better, achieve more in sports and at work, excel in exams, enjoy constructive relationships, overcome crises, and be sought out as a leader. All you need is to master Tactical Calm.

We laid the foundations in the last chapters. First, you have to know when you are on the wrong side of the curve. Second, you must be able to press the brakes with agility and skill. We don't want to skid or come to a stop. We want to move forward with control and confidence.

Drill 32: The rhythm of Tactical Calm

Recognise when you enter a challenging situation (speed).

Rapidly activate Tactical Calm (brake).

Relax into Flow under pressure (brake then accelerate).

Recover after focused effort (repair and maintenance).

Daily relaxation drills (tune your brakes).

The braking system requires the ventral vagus nerve. While these fibres are new in evolution, they are trainable. With practice, your vagus nerve becomes myelinated. Your brakes are well tuned. Repetition reinforces.

Tactical Calm is achieved through four systems:

1. Posture and hormones. In Freeze, you collapse or bow into submission. In Fight, you activate attack and lose your mental focus. In Flight, you pull away and run. In Tactical Calm, you remain relaxed with an upright, alert posture. The spine is long, the shoulders relaxed, head held high, and face relaxed. In this posture, testosterone increases (which is necessary for women as much as it is for men), cortisol decreases, and the vagus nerve fires. You feel relaxed, confident, clear, and present.

2. Breathing and heart rate. The physiology of Tactical Calm is to slow the heart rate, slow the breathing, and bring the heart into

alignment with the breath. This is called coherent heart rate variability.[42] When you breathe in, the heart accelerates slightly. When you breathe out, the heart rate slows.

3. <u>Emotion regulation.</u> While this sounds tricky at first, you counter fear with calm, anger with kindness, and sadness with joy. Emotions become your motivators. Positive emotions trigger coherent heart rate variability and improve your mind.

4. <u>Attention and presence.</u> Sympathetic activity initially focuses the mind but too much sends it into chaos. Thinking becomes disordered and unfocused. It is hard to see what is going on. Focus your attention on one thing: your breath, another person, a ball, a cloud, a flower, a candle, or your heart rate. Then open your mind to your senses and the full situation around you and within you; attention begets presence.

Drill 33: Clear insight

A powerful learning is to see if you can take one of the situations you described above in the chart and get a video (or an audio, although video is even better) of yourself. If you can't, see if you can ask someone to tell you what was happening. What did they notice about your posture, your breathing, your facial expressions, and your focus?

A cornerstone of Tactical Calm is heart rate variability (HRV). The concept is intimately related to posture, breathing rate, muscle tension and the parasympathetic system (vagal tone). You can measure HRV easily.

With slow, even breathing, you can control your heartbeat. In medicine, we call this Respiratory Sinus Arrhythmia (RSA). Slow diaphragmatic breathing enhances the effect. Your sympathetic and parasympathetic systems are evenly balanced.

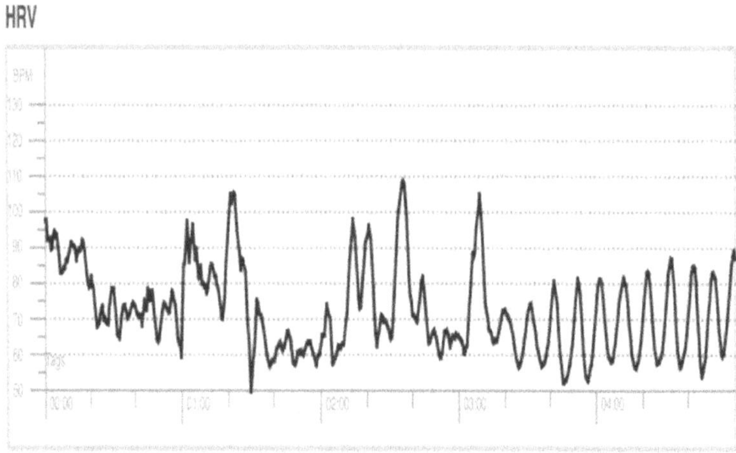

Figure 13: Heart Rate Variability: chaotic (0–3 min) and coherent (3–5 min)

The first three minutes above show a chaotic variation of heart rate between 50 and 110 beats per minute. This part of the curve is irregular and sharp with sudden rises and falls. Studies show this to be predictive of health risks including cardiovascular, inflammatory, and respiratory and mental illness, social disconnection, and cognitive failure. This chaotic pattern results when the sympathetic system dominates. Muscles tense, breathing becomes rapid and shallow, and adrenaline is active.

The recording after three minutes shows a coherent HRV between 50 and 80. The sine curve (smooth alteration of acceleration and deceleration of heart rate) is clear. The vagal brake is on. Parasympathetic balances the sympathetic surge.

Coherent HRV is strongly linked to health, emotional resonance, better brain function, and Bounce. It is a good example of homeostasis.

The change you see just past 3 minutes is Tactical Calm in action. At this point, the person feels calm, focused, and connected to the situation. The body, the emotions, and the mind work better. You are more able to tune into others with empathy.

The benefits of Tactical Calm are well demonstrated:

- Muscle relaxation, reversal of fibromyalgia (muscle pain)
- Slowing of breathing leading to optimised physiology and brain function
- Improvement in digestion and reduction of digestive/abdominal disorders
- Better blood flow to organs, particularly the skin
- Reduction of and ultimately removal of distress symptoms
- Reduced blood pressure and heart rate
- Improved immune system function and reduced inflammation
- Reduction in adrenaline, cortisol, and cholesterol
- Recovery from illnesses including heart disease, cancer, and asthma
- Better brain function, alertness, reaction time, and perception
- Reduction in anxiety, worry, and greater likelihood of a good night's sleep
- Improved mood, increased optimism, and sustainable happiness
- Improved concentration, executive functions, and memory.

If we can establish HRV coherence at will and at speed, we can master all kinds of difficulty. We also will be more healthy, happy, connected, intelligent, and creative. These are the positive outcomes of Tactical Calm practices.

Drill 34: Study your heart rate variability (HRV)

Take time to study your HRV. We prefer Heartmath's em-wave (www.heartmath.org). There are other apps. Practise establishing coherence.

Experiment and see which practice options work best for you. Select one that appeals. Invest at least five minutes per day. Over time you will find that you can activate Tactical Calm with speed. Your goal is to be able to activate the change immediately whenever a challenge presents.

Breathing with the diaphragm

Breathing is the most natural and intuitive living process. Breathing is unconscious and mediated within the brainstem in much the same way that temperature and blood pressure are controlled. While one can choose to stop breathing, once we lose consciousness, breathing will start again.

I learned last week that a participant in a CEO programme had committed to this practice. The next day, he got the horrifying news of a murdered son. He shared that it was the application of this breathing that got him through this tragic experience.

On average, humans today breathe 12 to 18 times per minute. Ideally, we breathe using the diaphragm. Under pressure, we activate the neck and shoulders more and diaphragm less.

As we inhale, the diaphragm contracts and pulls down, sucking air into the lower lungs. From the outside, it appears as if the ribs and belly are expanding with air. In fact, it is the diaphragm flattening and compressing abdominal contents down.

The air comes into contact with blood in the small alveoli of the lungs. Oxygen is absorbed into the blood for the production of energy and carbon dioxide diffuses back into the lungs for removal. The diaphragm then relaxes and comes up into the lungs, pushing air out.

Diaphragmatic breathing is a power lever to Bounce, Grow, Connect, and Flow.

> **Drill 35: Examine your breath**
>
> Examine your own breathing with the following exercise. Lie flat on your back. Place your right hand on your upper chest and the left hand between your belly button and lower ribs. Breathe normally and feel the flow of air. Which hand is moving more? For a few breaths, focus on breathing into the top of the chest so that your right hand moves more. Notice how your neck becomes stiff and your chest puffs out. Breathe in and out through your mouth. Breathe faster.

In distressed breathing, you are using the backup (or secondary) muscles of the neck and chest. It is inefficient and triggers distress. If you do this for too long, you become dizzy and confused, with tingling in your fingers and lips. We call this hyperventilation. Too much. Too fast. You reduce your blood carbon dioxide levels and create alkalosis (high pH).

You can observe this pattern in others. Breathing will be shallow and fast. Mouth breathing dominates. You can see the neck muscles activate and the upper chest rise. You will notice sighing and breath holding.

This pattern is common today under the relentless busyness of life. When we breathe like this, we will feel agitated, shut down to others, and unfocused. Performing at your best is simply not possible. Your heart is beating too fast, blood moves away from the brain and organs. If we breathe like this for long periods, we will become unwell.[43] Some are admitted to hospital.

Far too often, we hear or give the advice "take a deep breath". This is exactly the wrong advice as it activates the neck, chest, and mouth breathing.

Rhythm

To correct your breathing, you must slow it down to about six breaths per minute. You must breathe through your nose and keep the mouth closed. Soften the inhalation and lengthen the exhalation. The change immediately activates the ventral vagus nerve and improves oxygen transfer to muscle and brain. Carbon dioxide increases, stabilising the nervous system.

Drill 36: Correct your breathing

Again, lie flat on your back. Place your right hand on your upper chest and the left hand between your belly button and lower ribs. Breathe normally and feel the flow of air. For a few breaths, focus on breathing into the lower part of your chest and the abdomen so that your left hand moves more. Breathe smoothly through the nose (or a straw if you nose is blocked). Extend the exhalation to six seconds and breathe in very gently. Let the air flow in for about four seconds. Continue this slow even breath for five minutes.

Do you notice a difference? When we are relaxed and in our optimal performance zone, breathing is slow, low, even, and deep. If you are keen to advise others, may I suggest that you say:

- ☐ Breathe out.
- ☐ Exhale.
- ☐ When in doubt, breathe out.
- ☐ Let it go.

Distressed Breathing	Healthy Breathing
upper chest and collar bone lift and fall	lower ribs and belly expand and contract
uneven, sharp, and chesty airflow	low, slow, and even airflow through the nose
sharp inhalation—air grabbing	slow, smooth, and quiet inhalation
deep, audible sighs on exhalation	long, slow, quiet, and complete exhalation
tight belly and puffed chest	relaxed, soft belly and chest
stiff "military" or slouched posture	neutral posture, long and light spine
tight neck muscles, Dowager's hump	light, relaxed neck, ears over shoulders

Figure 14: Comparing distressed with healthy, rhythmic breathing

Rhythm

Basic Relaxation Practice

Basic relaxation practice is simple and easy to learn. The benefits can be experienced immediately. A first step is to create a period of at least five minutes where you can reduce external demands. The purpose is to reverse accumulated tension and fatigue, to rejuvenate your physical, emotional, and cognitive function, and to master the technique for quick and effective impact.

Drill 37: Deep relaxation practice

Lie flat on your back on the carpet or on a firm bed.

Tense each muscle group on the inhale.

Relax muscles fully on the exhale.

Progress from face, through body to feet.

Check that your entire body is soft and relaxed.

Focus between the ribs and the belly button.

Watch five breaths, observe pace, flow, and depth.

Lengthen the exhale to six seconds.

Soften the inhale to four seconds.

Soften the transition between exhale and inhale.

Relax and pause at the end of the exhalations.

Attend to your inhale with alertness and clarity.

Let your breathing be natural, soft, and unforced.

Release anxiety or frustration on the exhale.

Enjoy the freshness each inhalation.

End by extending the inhale and stretching.

Dr. Sven Hansen

Taking time to relax in our frantic lives never seems reasonable. Yet the science is clear, and the benefits follow quickly. So, build it into your day. Initially, five minutes at the end of the day—perhaps in preparation for connecting with family or partner—is ideal. It is also a great way to recover after strenuous sport.

Drill 38: Seated, quick relaxation practice

Keep your spine light and long.

Let your shoulders roll backward and down.

Breathe through your nose.

Relax your chest, and let your sternum sink downward.

Exhale completely over six seconds and pause gently.

Inhale slowly and evenly, aiming for four seconds.

Keep your chest, neck, and face relaxed.

Allow your belly and side ribs to expand.

Keep your face and neck relaxed.

Notice your pulse, muscle tone, and skin.

Take a few minutes, morning and night, to practice good breathing. Begin by sitting quietly in a chair with a straight back. Watch your breathing first. Observe where your muscles are tight, where you feel tension, and how your breath moves.

Then, slowly adjust your breathing practice to follow the instructions. Maintain your attention on the even flow of breath. Feel rather than force or think the breath.

Rhythm

Current research suggests that we should breathe about six times per minute (6 seconds out and 4 seconds in). Some suggest a fraction slower and balanced 5 and a half seconds in and out. Many techniques now suggest extending the exhale. Start with six seconds exhale and extend it up to fifteen. Make sure you are comfortable and extend only when it does not cause distress.

Training with HRV monitoring will accelerate your learning, confidence, and the benefits you achieve. You can watch your exhalations slow, and inhalations increase your heart rate. When you hyperventilate, the pattern becomes chaotic. As you restore a smooth, even diaphragmatic breath, coherence resurfaces.

If you are struggling, seek out a specialist for help. A breath-trained physiotherapist or competent yoga instructor can help. You will learn faster.

Drill this one. Specifically, remind yourself of it when sitting at traffic lights and stop signs, in meetings, when feeling anxious, or before an important event. As you improve, you will find that it is a powerful way to relax, calm anxiety, focus your attention, and ward off fatigue. It is also very helpful before falling asleep.

When competent, you can achieve rapid Tactical Calm in seconds. Simply exhaling for 10 seconds or slow breathing for a minute is enough.

Athletes, artists, and elite soldiers continuously use their breath to achieve their goals. You can do this too. With expertise, an intention in a moment can do the job. Your vagus nerve is myelinating. You have learned to use your vagal brake.

Breath Variations

For thousands of years, yoga and contemplative traditions have worked with breath as a focus for personal and spiritual development. Learn with a teacher. If meditation or mindfulness sounds weird to you, just breathe.

More recently, combat science has introduced and widely advocated the practice of Tactical Breathing. Also called Square Breathing, the goal is robust, quick, Tactical Calm in the heat of battle. The practice begins with four seconds exhalation, hold for four seconds, inhale smoothly for four seconds, and hold for four seconds. This has been shown to be highly effective when faced with deeply confronting challenges such as combat, sports, or stage performance.

Go back to your life situations with your breathing in focus.

- You have a bullet-proof path to Flow in your response to challenge. Drill it.
- Breathe out slowly through your nose for 12 seconds. Can you try15 seconds?
- Practice diaphragmatic breathing tonight to get into deep sleep. Don't forget!
- Practice the seated breathing when you are trying to concentrate. Drill it.
- Look for a scary challenge. Use your breath to master it. Drill it.

Rhythm

Tactical Calm is the Foundation of Meditation

Your Tactical Calm drills will open the door to contemplative practice or meditation. Meditation, contemplation, and mindfulness are cognitive practices. Tactical Calm is the base.

For now, extend your Tactical Calm or breathing practice. If you can accumulate roughly eight minutes per day, you will become healthier, calmer, more emotionally flexible, and more focused.

As you drill your diaphragmatic breath (physical), you can direct your attention to emotions or thoughts (mental). At first, simply notice. As you experience these activities of body, emotion, and mind, gently nudge yourself toward feelings of calm, appreciation, gratitude, and kindness.

Then you can move to directing your attention to be 100% focused on a point of breathing (for example, the flow of air at the nose, or the rise and fall of the belly).

Certain forms of meditation show impressive benefits to body, emotion, and mind[44] and are actively promoted by many highly credible scientists.[45] There are many options for meditation practice. A qualified teacher is recommended.

Drill 39: Establish a daily relaxation practice

Set aside 5 to 10 minutes for a daily practice of Tactical Calm. Ideally, prepare with some stretches, and then sit upright on a chair or cushion. Use the guidelines above to relax your body into a light, upright posture. Drop your attention to your breath. Watch the rise and fall. Lengthen the breath to 4 seconds in and 6 seconds out. Be relaxed, peaceful, and grateful. Steady your mind on your flowing breath. You are now meditating.

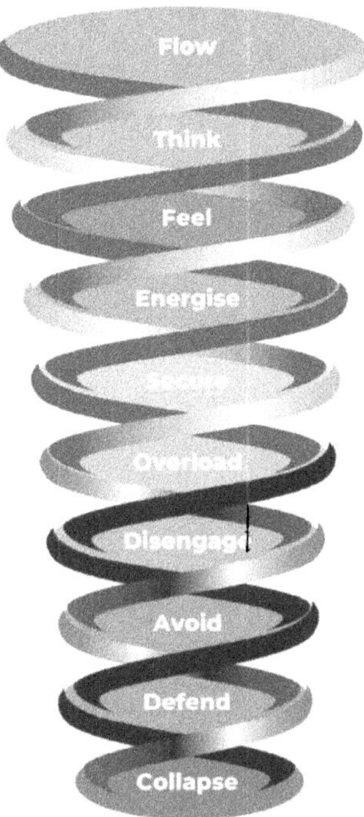

Figure 15: Review of the Resilience Spiral

Secure is the foundation of resilience and rhythm. Tactical Calm drills get you there. Think of Secure as the fulcrum for the rhythms of life and for homeostasis. It is the centre point of being safe, calm, present, and engaged.

When we extend ourselves as in training or confront an unwelcome adversity, we temporarily lose this Secure base. We long for this experience of being Secure. We use Bounce to get there faster.

At times we reach for the stars. We extend body, heart, and mind to find flow. This is exciting, fulfilling, and expensive activity. It requires training, discipline, and focus. Afterwards, we long to return to Secure. If we don't relax and recover, there is little prospect of rising to Flow tomorrow.

Biologists term this ebb and flow of life homeostasis.[46] Secure is the midpoint in a well-lived life. As you become more confident in your capacity to hold this state, life becomes a much more playful, productive, and joyous adventure.

When resilience fails, we lose confidence in our ability to maintain and cultivate this state. Secure is the foundation from which we can now explore how to awaken and master our physical, emotional, and cognitive resources.

Secure Leadership

The organisational equivalent of Secure is Safety. In many ways, this experience of safety is the foundation of culture, organisational effectiveness, and strategy. It is the first goal of leadership. When we experience a feeling of being safe and secure in a role and in the social networks of work, our potential is liberated.

When we don't feel secure or safe in a role or social network, we are thrust down the spiral. Wellbeing, trust, agility, and performance are out of reach. Instead, overload, disengagement, fear, anger, and resignation take hold of culture and work experience.

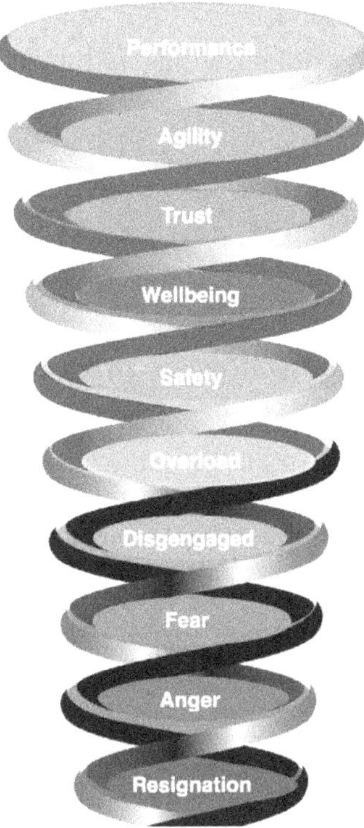

Figure 16: Review of the Organisational/Culture Spiral

With the rising incidence of attention disorders, autism, anxiety, and depression, young people are entering the workforce in various states of resilience failure. Thus, the explosion of interest in mental health at work. Ten years ago, few were interested.

As I write, the great resignation is in the media. Millions have chosen to leave or change jobs. Does that mean we have driven some to the bottom of the spiral?

If you are a leader, does that mean you have to be a therapist too?

How do you assign responsibility to individual or organisation?

If 20% of your organisation is anxious, is that your responsibility?

Rhythm

These are leadership concerns of our time. The answers are complex, and it will take time for organisations and their leadership to fully grasp and solve.

When a new employee joins with an anxiety disorder, the challenge of a new job will likely trigger more anxiety. That state of sympathetic activation, worry, rising panic, and avoidance possibly makes the experience of safety impossible—regardless of how effectively the organisation, leaders, and colleagues strive for it. When this person is diagnosed, put off work and treated, who exactly is responsible?

My recommendation to leaders is to get up to speed. First, you must educate yourself on the implications of wellbeing, resilience, and mental health in the workplace. These spirals and drills are a great place to start. Get to know how individual resilience becomes cultural resilience and how these affect your people and your business operations.

Second, you must find a way to measure what is going on for your people. Some will be thriving and finding flow, many will be secure, and some will be anxious, angry, or depressed. Just as we monitor machines, we now need to find respectful ways to monitor our people in ways that provide both individual and organisation clues to the next step on the Bounce, Grow, Connect, and Flow journey.

Securing yourself, your leadership team and your organisation at the Safety level is the foundation. Clear signals that you provide safety, clarity, and coherence to workers at all levels must be designed, orchestrated, and communicated in a consistent manner. It also goes without saying that you need to personally model all of this as much as you can. True leaders walk the talk.

The key factors in our experience include safety to tell the truth, insight to know your state, Tactical Calm, Bounce routines, and rhythm in daily work.

Summary

1. Clarify your explanation of relaxation, vagal brake, or Tactical Calm.
2. Breathe out long and slow.
3. Four seconds in and six seconds out—six breaths per minute.
4. Check your heart rate variability (HRV).
5. Define and consistently execute your own Tactical Calm practice.

Well done! This is challenging work. We have completed the first part of resilience which is the ability to Bounce forward fast when adversity strikes. In the next chapter, we move on to growing your physical vitality—sleep, fitness, breath, nutrition, and rhythm.

Part Three: Grow

The goal for Part Three is to develop your own practice of deliberate and effective Growth that brings you wellbeing, success, and happiness. Your challenge is to convert intention into precise and repeated actions to train the body, emotions, and mind.

The content here is stripped back to the core practices that will help you become that better (or best) version of yourself. As Anders Ericsson, whom we met in the first chapter, famously repeats: "Practice trumps intelligence every time."[47]

Finding the right way to put these practices into action in your own life is the surest way to build a structure for success. This may at first appear dull work—having to get up at a regular time, exercise daily, manage your emotions, and control your mind. But once you start to find a rhythm of daily practice, Growth begins to become easier and accelerate. Your abilities to Bounce, Grow, Connect, and Flow will find new energy and purpose.

The structure of Part Three is based on the three experiences of being a conscious human being: physical, emotional, and mental.

The body is our foundation. The human body with its 38 trillion (or thereabouts) cells is a magnificent creation of structure and function. We can work with its elasticity to nurture a long and satisfying life.

The emotions have more recently come into focus. While they are processed in the brain and become conscious in the mind, emotion is also a physical experience, so the body and emotions are connected. Simply remember a moment when you were head-over-heels in love, or in a panic, or in a panic about being in love. Emotion happens in chemicals, cells, muscles, and organs. We can tune into these experiences and consciously train them much like our muscles.

Finally, the mind perceives what is happening through the physical senses and the emotions. The mind helps us create meaning, construct alternative options, and make decisions. An undisciplined mind drags you into spirals of worry, resentment, disappointment, addiction, and failure. We can use the mind skilfully as the most powerful problem-solving system we know of.

Body Rules focuses on the body and what you need to build into your daily practices to be well-resourced physically. *Emotions Enrich* shows you how to engage with the rich and rewarding journey of emotional intelligence. *Mind Directs* will reveal how to understand, focus, and control your mind so it works for you, not against you. *Integral Daily Rhythms*, will show you how to put all this into practice in simple, deliberate steps that become a rhythm and even a ritual.

Body Rules

Your body is truly amazing. Your genetic code, cells, organs, bones, muscles, senses, nerves, and brain have evolved into a magnificent organism. Your body is designed to perceive, respond, move, feed, fight, rest, and reproduce. Bravo, Nature!

Yes, our genes code for the basic architecture and timed development schedule that takes us from fertilised egg to relatively helpless infant and on to functioning adult. The body dances in response to environmental signals, nurture by parents, play, social activity, and the efforts we put in to develop physical fitness.

We have comprehensive knowledge and practical options to help the body develop and thrive. We can complement the wonder of nature with a deliberate, guided, and individualised set of practices for each person.

Few own this responsibility and enjoy the fruits of physical wellbeing. Most of us are in terrible shape with an increasing gap every year between what we could be and what we are. The struggle to survive and earn money can remove the privilege of time to think about and invest in our health. Many prefer supplements, drugs, surgery, or magical solutions.

The "fix it" mindset abdicates us from responsibility and relies on skilfully marketed "fix it" solutions. Medical science, cosmetics, supplements, and scam artists are hungry predators for those with a quick-fix mindset.

In the past, nature was a demanding coach. If you did not get up early, others ate your breakfast. And if you really did not pay attention, you *became* breakfast. When you failed to take care of yourself, you could not find a mate. If you did not find a safe place to sleep at night, nocturnal predators removed you from the tribe and your genes from the pool.

The convenience and safety of our modern lives is an enormous leap of progress. Yet it has a downside. Nature as coach and fitness enforcer no longer keeps us in shape. Convenient consumption meets our every life desire. On average, we have become lazy, fat, sleep disrupted, dopamine addicted, and impulsive. Diabetes, heart and joint disease, cancers, ADHD, anxiety, and depression are our just rewards.

To move toward physical wellbeing, we have no option but to become our own coaches and fitness enforcers. Your body is the foundation of everything else. When the body is in good form, you will find the freedom and motivation to Grow and to develop your emotions and your mind.

There are few shortcuts. Perhaps coffee, blue/red berries, powernaps, sunscreen-free tanning (not in the middle of the day), and laughter serve as catalysts, but the rest is solid, steady work that lays the foundation of your rhythm to flourish and lead.

The goal of this chapter is to help you find a daily rhythm to take care of your body. The single greatest gift that parents (and possibly schools) could offer us, is to lay these foundations. If you are reading this book, you are probably well on your way. Repetition is good as every athlete knows. Drill, check, and drill again.

For many, the starting place is a world of pain. Most of us are wrestling the demons of sleep disruption, weight gain, injury, lack of basic fitness, anxiety (and disordered breathing), and a love-hate relationship with fast food. As such, rhythm is unlikely in your daily self-care practices.

The good news is, all of this can be enhanced, elevated, refined, and redesigned, and here's how:

First, fix your sleep.

Second, take care of your physical fitness.

Third, slow your breathing (see *Tactical Calm*).

Fourth, take charge of what you put in your mouth.

Fifth, build these healthful activities into a daily rhythm that works for you.

Sleep Mastery

We are waking up to the importance of sleep. In our most recent research report on 23,990 resilience assessments, *sleep quality ranked as the #1 most important factor in order to be in the top 10% of resilience scores*. A great read is Matt Walker's *Why We Sleep*.[48] There is wide acknowledgement that sleep is disrupted. The consequences are chilling. They undermine every aspect of a good life.

Adults get about an hour a night less than needed. Teenagers get almost two hours less than their critical development needs require. We go to bed too late and overstimulated. We sleep in to recover. We live perpetually jet lagged. Our timing and quality of sleep are disrupted from natural rhythms.

The consequences include: weight gain, diabetes, inflammation, heart disease, cancer, dementia, and attention disorders. Not to mention crankiness. Along with alcohol, fatigue is a major cause of road accidents, safety violations, and conflict. Sleep causes a loss of productivity estimated at 2-4% of GDP. Walker quotes studies showing costs to business of $1,400 USD per person per year as a consequence of sleep disruption. If you don't secure your sleep, your productivity is punished.

On the positive side, sleep is the ultimate performance and anti-aging treatment. Get a good night's sleep, and everything works better. You are a better version of yourself. You can jump higher, run faster, connect better, think smarter, and experience more joy.

We're taught to believe that everything goes better with Coke[R]! *Everything goes better with sleep.*

Food and water often have been in short supply through our

evolution. Hunger and thirst became powerful drives. Long, dark, cool nights and the danger of moving about in the dark meant that time for sleep was abundant through evolution. Compared with hunger and thirst, sleep is a weak drive.

Sleep is the most important element of rhythm. When your sleep rhythms are broken, every rhythm of body, emotion, and mind are disrupted. We must understand and master them.

There are three elements to lock in your sleep rhythm. Sleep timing, sleep need, and sleep quality. There is no prescription that will work for everyone. For genetic, environmental, work, and family reasons, you will have to experiment. Once you find what works for you, lock it into a non-negotiable routine.

Sleep timing helps you define the best times to fall asleep and to wake up each day. The circadian rhythm establishes the period during which sleep is most effective. When you sleep during the right hours for your personal clock, the quality of your sleep is optimised.

In humans, the circadian clock ranges from 24 hours to 25 hours. Sleep lags behind the 24-hour day-night cycle. There really are morning people and night people: larks and owls. A lark tends to have a short clock, thus gets tired early in the evening and is ready to get up early in the morning. The owl, with a longer circadian clock, gets tired later and prefers to sleep in through sunrise.

There is a dynamic relationship between the day-night rhythm and circadian clock. The primary rhythm is set by pre-sunrise blue light. Blue light reboots the active and alert period of your circadian rhythm through the supra chiasmatic nucleus behind the eyes.

The best way to stabilise your clock to the day-night rhythm is to get 20 minutes of pre-sunrise blue light. This becomes the foundational rhythm of all other biological rhythms. Physical activity, light, coffee or tea, social activity, refined carbohydrates, and mental habits can also adjust your circadian clock, for better or for worse.

Rhythm

Blue light in the evening will wake you up right when you need to prepare to sleep. We come home to blue LED lighting, TV screens, laptops, and mobile devices. In addition, we socialise, drink, and eat late. Your clock gets pushed toward later sleep onset.

Sleep Phase Delay is a common sleep disorder that pushes us to sleep too late. We are perpetually jet lagged and pressed into behaving more like an owl. There are established physical and mental health risks for the owl pattern. Recent studies show that there may be benefits to behaving more like a lark. This is certainly true for a lark and looks hopeful for the owl.

Beware of the weekend sleep-in. Roughly 30% of our clients sleep in later through the weekend to catch up on sleep. After a busy and sleep-deprived week, sleeping into the day allows your circadian clock to "free-run" a couple of hours into the next day. However, first, the quality of this "extra" sleep is poor. Second, it leaves you jetlagged through the next week. Because just as your body realigned the clock, you set it off track again.

What is the single most effective action to start with to improve your sleep timing? Wake up with or before dawn. Ideally be outside in dawn blue light. This is especially true on weekends. The best blue light is just before sunrise.

Tracey, a participant on a course some years back argued vehemently against losing the pleasure of a weekend sleep-in. Six months later, she grabbed my shoulder on a flight. She said: "When you explained the importance of wake-up times, I hated you. However, my husband and I have followed your plan. Our energy and our weekends have improved dramatically. Thank you".

Next, you must take care of the cool-down period. If you rise early and press into the night with blue-light stimulation, you will be sleep deprived. Sadly, many ask me what they can do if they cannot stare at and fidget on a screen.

Our needs are different. Here are my recommendations. I suggest that for an hour or preferably 90 minutes before sleep, you read a book, play a game (cards, jigsaws, board games), meditate, write (in a journal or notepad, not via a screen), talk, take a walk, stretch, take a bath, or make time for intimacy.

It is essential to avoid blue light from screens before sleep. Replace LED lighting with soft yellow lighting, and eat dinner early.

During this period, you want to shift heat from your core to your periphery. The body releases melatonin in the evening to help cool your core temperature slightly. When exposed to blue light, melatonin is compromised. An easy walk outside or a cool bedroom will help. Aim for 18 degrees Celsius (about 65 degrees Fahrenheit) or cooler if possible. Intense exercise in the four hours before sleep is not recommended as it increases your core temperature.

The final key is to apply your Tactical Calm techniques as you relax into sleep. Lie relaxed and flat on your back. Soften your face and chest. Breathe slowly, with your attention resting peacefully on the rise and fall of your belly.

Now let's look at the quantity of sleep. Sleep need is widely agreed to be somewhere between six and a half and eight hours. It is based on the S-phase, the requirement for the body to sleep for a period of each day. If we sleep too little or too much, the prospect of a good life declines fast. Every species has its own sleep need. We need more than most mammals our size. Our overdeveloped brain demands it.

Experiment and study your own requirement. The natural way is to go camping, live by natural light for three days and see what happens. Many people now use sleep trackers. Buy or borrow one and watch your sleep for a fortnight.

When you review the data on a sleep tracker, you will notice that your body keeps hunting for a consistent sleep period. Pay attention to how you feel when you get it and when you miss or exceed it. In my case the magic number is seven hours and twenty-two minutes. When I get it right, I feel refreshed. Too little or too much and I feel sleepy or lethargic.

Once you have established the right timing and protected your sleep need, the next challenge is to get your ultradian rhythm working. Think of this as your sleep-depth rhythm. The ultradian rhythm is a 90-minute cycle that allows for roughly two cycles of deep sleep followed by two or three cycles of dream sleep. When you get this right, the rejuvenation effects of sleep are optimised.

Simple trackers will give you an immediate, rough indication of your deep, light, and dream sleep. For an adult, approximately 25% of sleep is in deep or slow-wave sleep, 25% in dream or rapid eye movement (REM) sleep, and 50% in light sleep. Your teenager and child need more deep sleep as well as more sleep.

In the cycles of deep sleep that follow falling asleep, the brain and body are both quiet. Core body temperature drops. This is the time for repair and rejuvenation of cells. Growth hormone and testosterone production activates. The cardiovascular system slows right down. Immunity improves.

In light sleep, the body is more active and in transition.

During the dream cycles through the early morning hours, the brain is active while the body is paralysed. If not, we might act out our dreams and sleepwalk. Dreaming sleep facilitates memory, learning, creativity, emotional intelligence, and recovery from traumatic experiences.

Deep sleep is prioritised if you are deprived of sleep. The best deep sleep comes in the 10 p.m. to 2 a.m. period. As we get older, deep sleep is less effective. Securing the best deep sleep one can is an effective longevity tactic.

Late nights compromise your dream sleep cycles. To reduce mental illness and anxiety in young people, an obvious first step is to help them get to sleep earlier so that they complete their dream sleep. Quality sleep will reduce the suffering caused by attention disorders, anxiety, and depression. As parents we have two key responsibilities to our children. First, get devices out of bedrooms, and second, maintain a regular, blue-light infused wake-up time.

There will be times when healthy sleep is disrupted. Accept this calmly and make it up quickly. The best solution if you need to repay sleep debt is to go to bed the next night an hour or so early. Eat early or eat less at night. Remove all devices, cool the room, and read a book.

Finally, a short powernap of ninety seconds to fifteen minutes is another effective way to catch up on sleep. Ideally, the best time is just after lunch. Find a private, quiet, cool, and dark place. Set an alarm. Use your breathing to drop off more quickly. If sleep does not come, simply enjoy the rest.

Drill 40: Secure the foundation of rhythm: your sleep

Explore and track your sleep need, timing, and quality.

Wake up and go outdoors for 20 minutes before sunrise.

Never sleep in. Never snooze. When you wake, get out of bed.

Create a cool, quiet, yellow-light evening environment.

Avoid all screens 90 minutes before sleep.

Let your body cool before sleep.

Engage your diaphragmatic breathing practice.

Enjoy nature's gift of deep, quality, and unbroken sleep.

Rhythm

Physical Fitness

The second step for the body is to establish your exercise rhythms. Through evolution, we averaged 9 to 15 km of brisk walking per day with added digging and climbing. Modern and widely promoted advice is to get at least 30 minutes of moderate activity per day. Globally, 75% of us fail to meet this humble guideline.

Our research shows that fitness is the sixth most important factor for overall resilience. And overwhelming evidence demonstrates that physical fitness is the single most powerful intervention to reduce suffering, improve wellbeing, increase lifespan, and boost productivity.[49]

The combination of movement and rest, along with sleep, embed rhythm into our biology. Modern, sedentary lifestyles crush these rhythms. Physical activity is sacrificed. Biology is disrupted, wellbeing is compromised, and health fails.

My wife and I walk briskly along the beach almost every morning. Over the years, I have met dozens of clients on this walk who have added this simple daily discipline to their day. Their gratitude is humbling. A small change can drive significant transformation in your energy, fulfilment, and productivity.

Daily exercise is also a strong stimulus for improved quality of sleep. There are unlimited options to solve your exercise needs; many good resources are available. Brisk movement will take care of your cardiovascular and aerobic systems. Stretching will protect your muscles, joints, and movement even in old age. Strength, also known as resistance training, maintains your muscle mass. Posture and balance are essential to life functions and your impact upon others. If you want a boost, add two bursts of high intensity activity per week.

Experiment with different options. Train with friends, or join a club or gym. Test the best times for your body and lifestyle. When you find elements that leave you feeling great afterwards, embed them into your rhythm.

Enough said. Get this done.

<table><tr><td>

Drill 41: Integrated exercise rhythm example

Stretch every morning for at least 5 minutes.

Deepen your breathing, and exhale for 10 seconds into each stretch.

Balance for 30 seconds on each foot with eyes closed. Keep a hand close to a support until confident.

Schedule at least 30 minutes of activity (your pleasure) 6 days per week.

Twice a week do some resistance training—squats, press ups, sit-ups, etc.

Twice a week get in a challenging burst such as sprinting up stairs.

</td></tr></table>

Breath

The third element of rhythm is breath. We fully explored this above in *Tactical Calm*.

I have witnessed thousands of our clients find practical relief and benefits from establishing a daily rhythm of breathing practice. Aim to accumulate eight minutes of deliberate, precision breathing daily.

Just in case, the practices are summarised below. Try one right now.

Drill 42: Daily breath control rhythms

Add long, slow, and full breathing to your stretch routine.

Sit or lie down and practice diaphragmatic breathing for five minutes.

At the end of each burst of work or activity, breathe slowly for one minute.

Exaggerate your breathing—full or long—at least once a day to energise.

Use your diaphragmatic breathing before sleep.

Nutrition

While nutrition is important, it gets more attention than it deserves. If we are physically active, sleeping well, and remaining calm and rhythmic, many of the current eating disorders that plague modern life will drop away.

When you ask more of your body, it will demand better quality food and burn the excess quietly in the background. If you get your sleep sorted, cravings will reduce, and appetite regulation normalises. Just one weekend sleep-in (social jet lag) is known to increase the craving for and consumption of high-calorie foods. Mental illness and distress are well-recognised triggers for abnormal eating behaviours.

Food is visual, tangible, audible, aromatic, and tasty. Food has effects on our conscious and unconscious states. The food industry has mastered the ability to target these impulses and drive eating behaviours for profit rather than health. In short, we live in a toxic food environment.

There are many ways to improve nutrition so that it contributes to your wellbeing. The first step is to increase your awareness of your food impulses. Name the experience of craving for what it is—an aberrant addiction.

The second step is to learn to shut your mouth and redirect yourself if a brief examination of the need, value, and risk does not stack up.

The third step is to stay close to nature. Seek good soils, limited chemicals, biodiversity, home gardens, fresh and unprocessed foods. Eating that which is not destroyed by processing will improve nutrient density, fibre, gut bacteria, immunity, gut health, mood, and many factors that shaped our evolution.

These basic steps of awareness plus restraint plus nature will solve most food issues. For some, the transition to more natural foods needs to be gentle and slow. If you can master the drama of food, you will be well prepared to attend to the drama in your emotions and mind.

There are many ways to eat well. We must each find the rhythm that best suits our personal, family, and activity needs. As I see it today, Mediterranean, Asian, Vegetarian, and Low-Carbohydrate diets seem to work best.

You may also want to try keeping a food log for a couple of weeks and avoid allergens such as gluten, dairy, eggs, soy, and corn, and reintroduce them one at a time. Many people have undiagnosed food sensitivities, and they can change over time. We have long recommended some very simple principles to guide healthy eating.

Drill 43: Basic principles behind a sensible eating rhythm

Select, prepare, and eat a wide range of colourful vegetables (9 servings).

Drive your sugar and refined carbohydrate consumption down firmly.

Balance your plate with protein, healthy fats, and vegetable fuels.

Try intermittent fasting or a ketogenic (healthy fat) diet.

Take time to eat slowly and joyfully with family and friends. Be relaxed and grateful.

In concluding this chapter, you have the foundations for a rhythm that will build your resilience. These include recognising your altitude, welcoming adversity, identifying resilience failure, bouncing forward rapidly, mastering Tactical Calm, staying physically active, sleeping well, and eating a prudent diet.

This is where our clients make meaningful gains. These steps are well established, evidence-based, safe, and practical. When you build these foundations into your daily practice and execute them in a disciplined way, your life will surge up the spiral.

If we want to tackle preventable disease, poverty, inequality, and mental illness, this is where the emphases must be. The overall gains to community, businesses, and nations are hopelessly neglected.

Two encouragements. First: Approach your journey of change from the perspective of rhythm. These foundation rhythms will nurture you in thousands of different ways. The rhythms of stretch and relax, exhale and inhale, focus and refuel, heart rate variability, sleep, move, and recover are the orchestra.

Your job is to conduct the different rhythms into the performance of each day. The conductor has experience with different composers and styles of music. They know their music well. They practice the timing diligently. A masterful performance of music is ultimately a rhythm that integrates the different elements with precise timing. Just like your favourite music, the impact of daily rhythms can be felt immediately. The benefits steadily increase over time.

Look at your daily diary to schedule the best times for your non-negotiables. From the time you commit to get up. Put in time for each of the elements. If you are a lark, start early. If an owl, start a bit later. Most evidence suggests that the morning is the best time to chunk in the key elements.

For example, I am always out of bed by 4:45 a.m. By 7 a.m., I have completed a set of stretches, balance exercise, breath control and meditation, and 30 minutes of aerobic activity in blue light. If I am under time pressure, I do a short burst of more intense strength or speed work instead.

Get this planned and start immediately. Everything else from here on depends upon these foundations.

Second: Don't leave execution to chance, and don't delay. Get started today. Start with one or two things and be content if it is just a few minutes. As the discipline becomes a habit—like cleaning your teeth—it becomes rhythmic and natural. Your body, emotions, and mind will demand it.

If you are uncertain about your ability to execute, pair up with a good friend, join a club or group, or hire a coach. Over the years, the support of my paddling, swimming, and kite-surfing groups has been essential to maintaining my rhythms. When life is demanding, the last thing you want to do is exercise. Knowing that you have others to share the experience with motivates you to engage. The physical, social, and emotional benefits of shared activity will likely become a great source of joy.

Rhythm

Stay alert to the activities that feel good and leave you with an afterglow. There is no need to do things you hate. Habit, discipline, friendship, and enjoyment will help you launch a rhythm that moves you up your spiral.

We all have experienced the constraint of lockdowns through Covid-19. The normal rhythms of life and work were significantly disrupted. In times of adversity, daily rhythm becomes even more essential to our wellbeing, mental health, and productivity. Different situations will call for different rhythms. Be creative in testing variations.

When we face natural disasters or mass trauma, rhythm is at the top of the list for recovery, healing, and prevention of mental illness.

Mastering your rhythm with young children at home, or a partner who is not on board with your changes, is a very different challenge to being single or retired. Your optimal rhythms need to change over time. Express your needs, negotiate, and stand strong for healthy boundaries. You need to take care of you, no matter who you live with or what they are doing. You can do this!

Drill 44: Establish your daily practice rhythm

Be curious: examine the rhythms of those you respect.

Pencil in some daily time slots for each element.

Focus on what will give you the biggest benefit.

Invest in coaching, learning, or mastering new skills.

Give yourself a timeframe to launch new layers.

Life throws curveballs. Don't beat yourself up. Repeat.

Enjoy one of the greatest investments in your life.

In summary, define and master the drills that support you best. Then establish the rhythm of these drills into each day. Sleep, Flow, Bounce, relaxation, focus and exercise are not negotiable. As you execute rhythm with precision, you will feel cadence (a rhythmic sequence). Cadence leads to momentum. Momentum supports flow.

When adversity strikes, such as financial crisis, epidemic, or war, it is this daily rhythm that enables you to Bounce, Grow, Connect and discover your Flow. We will revisit these rhythms at the end of Part Three.

Next up is emotion and how to build your emotional intelligence.

Emotions Enrich

The goal of this chapter is to understand and master emotion. Emotion has been essential to life since the earliest organisms billions of years ago. Emotion moves us away from suffering and towards pleasure.

The emotional drive to reduce human suffering has stimulated medicine and healthcare. The desire for pleasure drives the splendour of modern art, music, and sport. It also facilitates the seductive trap of addictive substances from junk food to alcohol and opioids.

Without the stormy passions of emotions, life is terribly dull. In fact, life would unravel and come to a stop. The Latin word *movare* means "to move". A variation *emovare* means "to move or displace". Emotion moves us. Emotion drives life, evolution, and innovation. Emotion drives our bodies, minds, and actions.

If we fail to respond to pain and pleasure, we become numb and lose the drive to survive and prevail. We sink into a morbid depression.

Darwin laid the foundations for research on emotions 150 years ago. Yet only in the last 30 years has the world of emotion become widely available for study and application. Emotion remains a mysterious and uncomfortable topic for many. We frequently hear a despairing sigh from groups starting this training module.

Great artists created their work to stimulate the emotions of the audience. The masters like Shakespeare, Mozart, and Michelangelo applied the subtleties of emotion with expertise. It is unsurprising that many of the great creatives suffered from emotional dysregulation common in depression and bipolar disorders.

As early pioneers in emotional intelligence like Daniel Goleman and Richard Boyatzis showed, 85% of outstanding leadership is based on emotional rather than cognitive competencies.[50] If we want to transform ourselves and improve the experience of life for others, emotional energy is essential.

Finally, most of emotion is not consciously available. When we become aware of emotion, we can call it a feeling and name it. We perceive it subjectively as an experience we are having. The feeling is a mental image that is available for examination. Just like a food object, we can explore and assess the emotion and then decide if it is fit for consumption.

That is the crucible of enlightenment. Perhaps Socrates might have said, "The unexamined emotion is not worth having".

Many business leaders like to advise: "Keep emotion out of it!" They could not be more wrong.

The Biology of Emotion

The first step in mastering emotion is to educate yourself on the facts. Emotions are not soft and fluffy. They are hard, objective, and robust operations in living systems. Emotions explode in the body in measurable change. These include changes in heart rate, blood pressure, blood chemistry, blood flow, neural circuits, viscera, muscle tone, posture, tone of voice, and facial expression.

Imagine you have a near-miss incident on the road. You nearly killed yourself/your family. During the experience, the emotion and physiology of fear surges in your body. At first, you are not aware of it. The cardiovascular, chemical, neurological, visceral, and muscle changes happen faster than your conscious awareness can track.

Extreme fear can disable the body, distort thinking, and drive irrational actions. Muscle can be so stiff that you steer straight into the crash or so reactive that you swerve violently causing the car to roll.

If you are lucky, the other driver takes skilled evasive action. You feel shaken. You sense tension in your legs and lower back, thumping of your heart, and a bloodless face. It is intense.

It takes time to calm down enough to rationally comprehend the experience. The way you process the experience is critical to your long-term recovery. You might conclude that driving is life threatening and thus you never drive again—a kind of post-traumatic stress reaction. When you enter a car, you feel overwhelming fear.

Alternatively, you resolve to join a defensive-driving course. You apply the experience to stimulate adaptive learning.

Flight (fear), Fight (anger), and Freeze (immobilise) are coded emotional reactions that evolved to protect us.

All living systems swing from actions to counter suffering to those that secure pleasure. Quenching thirst, finding good food, or connecting with others feels good. These positive emotions are temporary. We swing back to calm.

Neurologist Antonio Damasio[51] shows how homeostasis is fundamental to all life—we seek to avoid suffering and maximize pleasure. Without it, life cannot prevail. What bacteria can do is basic, but their actions are still guided in a way that protects and secures life. What we can do with complex nervous systems and conscious, regulated emotions is a symphony in comparison.

The bacterium is not conscious. It has no nervous system to view an image of fear with awareness. Damasio argues that it has an unconscious feeling that triggers action. As nervous systems evolve from nets to spinal cords and brains, organisms have greater awareness and a wider range of options available. Life gets interesting.

Human brains, nervous systems, circulation, musculature, and endocrine systems have allowed this ancient sensing and feeling system to develop into the world of conscious and regulated emotion. This is the foundation of knowing and consciousness as Damasio describes.

We are not bacteria or reptiles. Every human can wake up to emotion. If you choose not to embrace emotion, you are opting out of humanity and choosing a reptilian existence. Not smart.

Scientists argue about how many emotions we have. Paul Ekman focused on the seven primary emotions: fear, anger, sad, happy, surprise, disgust, contempt. Simon Baron-Cohen has advocated for 412 mutually exclusive emotions. These are arranged in 24 groups at six levels of subtlety. For example, rage is extreme whereas feeling irritated, impatient, or dismissive are more subtle.

Simply defining emotions with a clear description and context is liberating. Without the description, emotion feels like a messy, uncomfortable, and uncontrollable experience. When you give it a name, you can work with clarity.

Regardless of your preferred framework, study and learn these emotions. Paul Ekman's website, www.paulekman.com is a great starting point. Emotions are objective patterns seen across all humans. The pattern of an emotion is seen in the face and posture, heard in tone of voice, and measured in the dynamics of circulation, autonomic nervous system, and chemical milieu. A computer can capture these signals with greater accuracy than most humans.

This knowledge is the source of emotional intelligence. Application provides the focus and flexibility for creative solutions to life's challenges. There's no time to lose. Without this knowledge, we are reacting much like a bacterium. Humans are the only species able to build this knowledge consciously and deliberately.

Mastering Emotion

Once consciously aware of emotion, the door opens to mastery. We can regulate emotion with skill. Imagine if you could choose to activate curiosity when afraid, or love when angry. This is the key to reduce suffering and optimise joy.

When we are reactive or impulsive, strong emotions are triggered that over-ride thought and skill. These are the Flight (panic), Fight (rage), and Freeze (tears) reactions that also have been called amygdala hijacks. They are defined in a sequence of trigger event, instant reaction, strong emotion, and regret.

Rhythm

As we described in *Bounce Forward Fast*, our job is to ***name them, tame them, and reframe them***. With full emotional mastery, we can work beyond the simple drills and build the emotional flexibility that creates a good life, strong relationships, and effective leadership. This can only be done with the application of your mind—a tricky character you will meet in the next chapter.

The door to emotional mastery also requires the foundations discussed so far in this book. Altitude, Bounce, Tactical Calm, breath control, and physical wellbeing.

You know this. A bad night's sleep, hangover, missed meal, or family conflict can drop us into explosive and destructive amygdala hijacks.

The next step is to drill emotional awareness. Keep a journal of the feelings you experience each day. Describe the situation, the physical experience of the feeling, and the accompanying thoughts. Reading good fiction is another way to broaden your awareness of emotional experience. Watching movies and stopping to discuss emotional scenes can be as enlightening as it is entertaining.

Bring emotion actively into your conversations. Explain how you are feeling. Ask others how they are feeling. Explore possibilities together.

Meditation practice is recommended by almost every expert in the field as a way to view, accept, and master your experience of emotion. It is a good way to build your awareness and mastery of emotion. Remember that emotions move us—often unconsciously. In meditation you learn to observe emotion in detail. You learn to enjoy the richness of feelings without being compelled to react to them. There is real power here.

You have brought emotional awareness into play. It is a lifelong journey of evolving depth and richness. As you deepen your practice, you will start to notice the motivations that arise from emotion. As you feel fear, you can sense a desire to avoid. When you feel anger, you can sense a desire to strike out or hurt. When you feel joy, you can sense a desire to connect and celebrate.

Drill 45: Explore and savour your emotions

Ask what you are feeling, and name your emotions as they arise.

Keep a journal describing strong emotional events from the day.

Read good fiction and enjoy film and theatre, noticing emotions.

Bring emotions and feelings into your conversations.

Meditate daily and pay attention to your feelings.

Cultivate a positive emotion, or gratitude, with each breath.

With time, you will be able to name your emotions and fully embrace the pressures they exert to act. Pause, accept, pay attention, and examine the consequences.

You are on the brink of freedom. When hijacked, there is no choice. Suddenly you are shouting or crying. With emotional awareness, you calmly pay attention to the emotional drama. You will recognise the patterns. You may be shocked that you have a choice. You can walk away from a conflict. You can evaluate your options to engage. You can carefully consider the best way to solve the conflict.

You are ready to be a force for good, in your own life and in influencing others constructively. It is this awakening that I believe is changing the course of humanity. This enlightenment is well on its way. It may take a few more centuries but ever greater numbers of people are crossing the threshold.

The final step to building your capacity for emotional mastery is emotional gymnastics. The figure below shows you how to identify, counter, and master impulsive emotions. Just as gymnasts strengthen muscles and develop grace and power, so too you can strengthen the power of positive emotion within you.

Drill 46: Emotional gymnastics

This table will help you use your growing awareness of emotions to practise countering negative emotions with more positive ones.

Impulse	Counter	Open	Grow	Radiate
Fear	Breathe out	Relax	Embrace present	Equanimity
Craving	Laugh	Detach	Contentment	Gratitude
Sadness	Acknowledge	Be Curious	Appreciation	Joy
Anger	Accept	Respect	Kindness	Altruism
Fatigue	Own it	Engage	Energise	Passion

Figure 17: Emotional gymnastics: turning the energy of destructive emotion to positive.

Dr. Sven Hansen

There are many ways to do this. Construct a process that works for you. Let's take the craving example. The craving impulse is most likely in the Disengaged state. The mind is tired, focus is distracted, and blood sugar may be low. An image of chocolate, wine, or tobacco lights up in the mind with a strong craving.

If you have an addiction, you know that the impulse urgently compels you to secure the dopamine hit. It is very serious. Here are a few alternatives that can really help:

- Counter it with laughter. Watch a funny video or comedian. Read a humorous book. Use this distraction to detach from the craving (tame it).
- Remind yourself how content you could be. Visualise profound contentment, right here, right now, or with your imagination. Activate gratitude that you were able to identify, engage and transform the impulse to something much more enjoyable.

It is this very process that the happiest people follow. Buddhism and Laughter Yoga have specific routines to help you build the muscles required. While emotions can feel like tidal waves, with training they become quieter. You can learn to surf them. Surfing is all about rhythm—anticipate the wave, prepare, pick up the energy, and ride it creatively.

When you can move from impulse to radiating a powerfully positive alternative at speed, you are enlightened. It's that simple.

By the way, fulfilment is the second highest-ranked factor that defines the top ten percent of resilience scores.

Truth is, this is hard work. There is nothing like a family problem, health issue, or traffic jam to remind you how long the journey can be.

In my own practice, I find a simple daily routine very helpful. After stretching and breath training, I focus on building a wave of positive emotion. With the first breath, I generate calm, the second passion, third loving kindness, fourth contentment, and fifth radiant joy. You can substitute other emotions, whatever you need in the moment.

Amplify the positive emotion on each inhalation, and radiate it outwards on each exhalation. Gently note and release negative feelings and thoughts that arise. Bring your awareness back to the positive feeling. By choosing a positive emotion as a focus for your breathing practice, you invoke a positive experience that will stay with you after the practice.

Drill 47: Positivity bench press

Establish a daily relaxation or meditative practice.

Stretch out all muscle groups for five minutes.

Breathe slowly using Tactical Calm for three minutes.

Focus on positive emotions (calm, passion, love, contentment, or joy).

Generate the maximum volume of each emotion on inhale.

Radiate that positive emotion to the world on exhale.

To maintain your range of positive emotions, focus on a different emotion each day. For example:

- ➢ Monday: calm and secure
- ➢ Tuesday: energy and passion
- ➢ Wednesday: love and kindness
- ➢ Thursday: contentment and clarity
- ➢ Friday: joy and fulfilment

Learning to accept and work skilfully with emotion takes time and deliberate attention. Be patient, the reward is worth it. In the next chapter, we will address the mind and thinking. It is only when the body and emotions are mastered that the full power of thinking becomes available.

Mind Directs

The mind is often overrated. For most of us it is the 'drunken monkey' that dredges up a storm of thoughts that can wreck your wellbeing and cause untold suffering. Anyone who has experienced depression or anxiety knows how repetitive and destructive thoughts can invade consciousness.

The brain itself, which is part of the body, with cells, blood flow, chemicals, and electrics, is one magnificent construction. It has been built up over billions of years from simple neural nets, adding spinal cord, reptilian, and then mammalian structures.

The modern human brain has had to sacrifice many of the older structures, to pack in the neocortex that allows for enhanced perception, creativity, judgement, language, and complex social interaction. When I need hope for humankind, I reflect on this amazing construction and the wonders it can produce.

The brain is built to operate a moving organism. It can map itself in an environment with exquisite complexity. It works out what is required to survive or thrive and develops complex plans to achieve these goals. It executes with wonderful precision and flexibility.

This messy biological activity gives rise to the experience of mind in humans and perhaps in some other species.

For this chapter, I define the components that are trainable with widely accepted benefits: self-awareness (know your mind), attention control (focus), and situational agility (adaptability).

Know your mind

Metacognition (insight or consciousness) is being alert to the content of your mind. The mind creates images sourced in the experience of life. These thoughts include *I am running, I am hungry, I am writing an e-*

mail. They are in the present moment. Antonio Damasio calls them the feeling of being.[52]

The source of these images includes the environment (hot, someone shouting), and an internal milieu of feelings from the viscera (anxious, hungry), sight, sound, smell, touch, and taste. These images are processed in the brain's sensory regions and in the anterior insula and cingulate gyrus. The images are brought together in convergence zones within the brain to create experience.

As humans, we can focus on this experience and create a story to describe what is going on. For example, *I am hungry because I missed breakfast and smell bacon.* We are aware of the experience. This is perception.

There is huge variation in this metacognition. While some cannot feel their heartbeat, others experience it as a hammering in the chest. There are risks to both extremes. Emotional states will mute or amplify the volume of certain signals.

We draw on memory and future planning to create an autobiographical self. This is the story of your life placed on a timeline. As far as we know, only humans can do this. For example, *I am always hungry and cranky if I don't eat in the morning. I should eat breakfast, I love bacon, but it will make me fat.*

The images provided by the brain to consciousness become thought. We conclude that we are thinking this or that. In the example above, the "story" is available to help us make life decisions. Depending on the goal you focus on, you may decide to eat bacon, delay breakfast, eat something else, or choose to take a walk.

It is estimated that we have 6,000 to 70,000 thoughts per day. Whatever that number is for you, it is a lot of noise. Unfortunately, many of these thoughts can be dull, repetitive loops.

When fuelled by fear or anxiety *(I am starving)*, your mind can generate floods of worries concerning how you are going to get food to survive. These worries may crowd out awareness of what else might be going on. In anxiety, we create a vicious cycle of worry and fear. Metacognition fades out of consciousness.

If we are fuelled by anger (*Why didn't he offer me breakfast?*), the mind will generate thoughts about why this is not fair, how awful the person is, and how you might get revenge. This rumination on the past wrongs of others creates waves of anger and resentment. Anger can fester, generating a frustrated and hostile experience of life, or it can burst out as rage.

When fuelled by sadness or disappointment (*I am such a fat loser*), the rumination focuses on your own past wrongs. Repeated loops of self-abuse, sadness, and despair can crowd out all sense of joy, hope, and fulfilment. This is the experience of depression.

Thinking is a wonderful tool, but it often goes astray. Until or unless we learn to master it. Cognitive Behaviour Therapy (CBT) took advantage of this in the 1960s. It has proven to be a powerful healing approach for depression, anxiety, and hostility. The foundation of CBT is that we must learn to be fully aware of our thoughts. When we see the content of a thought, we can step back and examine both its accuracy and utility, and we can replace it with a more useful, empowering thought if it is not serving us.

Metacognition is the foundation for skilful thinking. Do not trust your mind. It is, as the mystics would say, a drunken monkey. This monkey must be seen for what it is, challenged, restrained, and trained into better behaviour. This can only be done with deliberate attention to the content of your thoughts.

Drill 48: Identify and define your thoughts

Add a daily reflection on your thoughts to your journal.

Select one or two notable thoughts to work on.

Define the exact words that your mind generated.

Write them down.

Note the associated feelings.

Reflect on the accuracy and utility of the thought.

Adjust as needed.

When we name our reactive behaviour or emotions, it removes the potency and tames them. To name your thoughts removes their stickiness and persistence. This is an important aspect of meditation practice.

In meditation you sit quietly and relaxed and simply notice, without judging, the content of your mind. For example, *Oh, I am thinking about food. Let's go back to my breath.* We calmly notice, we name, and we release the thought. This is the essence of self-awareness practice. Meditation helps us become more attentive to the activity of our mind.

In time, thoughts that bother you simply fade away. They are less interesting and less compelling. You might note, perhaps even humorously, that these thoughts are boring and rather stupid.

A critical transition is happening. You are moving from thought being the subject to thought being the object. When caught up in a worry cycle in the early hours of the morning, it feels like a storm. You identify with it. You are the storm. Then as you pay attention to the thought, by having a "meta thought", you have made that thought an object of awareness. You witness it. The thought is no longer you. It is just your mind trying to make sense of experience.

You shift from *I am this thought* to *That is not who I am. That is just my thinking in this moment. This too shall pass. I notice and let it go.*

There is distance between the experience and the mental activity. You have discovered the conscious state of self-awareness. You are free to choose. You can let the thought subside, you can challenge it, or you can select a more helpful thought.

As you get comfortable paying attention to your thoughts, you will be able to catch unhelpful thoughts not only when you are meditating, but throughout the day; and you will be empowered to let them go or replace them.

To do this well, we move to Attention Control.

Attention Control

Attention control or focus is deciding to direct your mind with conscious intent. Once you have clear insight or perception into the activity of your mind, you have the choice to direct your mind. Just as you can choose to flex a muscle to lift an object, or you can generate an emotion that motivates an action *(I am going to be so amazing today, and this will be fun!)*, so you can focus and hold your attention on a selected experience or action.

As Johann Hari describes in *Stolen Focus*[53], we live in a world of densely packed, high-velocity information. Every media format, app, advertisement, and product is designed to grab our attention and activate the dopamine circuit of desire. He concludes from interviews with experts that the average adult switches attention every 3 minutes. Younger people switch every 18 or 19 seconds.

This is a foreign environment for the human brain which was designed to pay attention to the slow rhythms of hunter-gatherer life.

Rhythm

Attention is disrupted. Attention disorders are normal. We desperately stimulate focus with caffeine, sugar, and Ritalin. This costly switching of attention has overwhelmed the default mode network we described in Bounce.

The result is a mind that has lost the depth and duration of attention (deep focus) needed to achieve our goals. *I'm writing with focus. Oops, better check the markets. Maybe check that email. No, I'll make tea.* Once disturbed, to get back into writing Flow can take thirty minutes. How many times will I interrupt myself in those thirty minutes? It's amazing anything ever gets done. The intensity and control required for deep and productive work in Flow is rare.

Drill 49: Protect your brain and your mind

Switch off all notifications on all devices.

Switch off phones, internet, and media feeds when completing a task.

For deep work in Flow, remove these devices from sight.

Open one programme on your screen at a time.

Choose your meeting environment for peace and quiet.

Avoid TV screens at work or during family time

Connect online in short, focused bursts, perhaps four times a day at set times.

To solve the challenges of modern life, we must wage war against distraction. This is the first level of attention control. Johann Hari takes us on his rather amusing journey to escape distraction. Try losing weight in a bakery. We can retreat to a monk's cave, we can switch off our notifications, smash our phones, or purchase a stack of productivity tools. Removing distractions is important but not enough.

So, let's take a look at real solutions to master your mind.

Once we remove distractions, the second level of attention control is to make sure your brain has the reserves for deep focus. Quality sleep is essential. So is regular, rhythmic rest. We have talked about the default mode network. This is the mental activity associated with rest. Fiddling on your device is not rest. Taking a walk outside or closing your eyes for a few diaphragmatic breaths is quality rest.

As we discussed, there is a rhythm between focus and rest. Find the right rhythm to switch from focus into that default mode network on a regular basis through the day. Explore how long you need to rest and recover between focused bursts of work.

Daily exercise, upright posture, and good levels of fitness are proven to improve the quality of attention. Good nutrition that removes sugar spikes and dips is also useful. Some find the low-carbohydrate, high-protein approaches helpful. Finally, your emotions must be in check and mostly positive.

Remembering the monkey mind, we must identify unhelpful worry and rumination. Note it, then return to your point of focus (breath, movement, work, tree, positive thought, etc.). Keep your attention in the present moment. If you are caught up in mindless concerns about the past or the future, your mind is not available for the present.

Deep focus is 100% present to the moment.

In the manic work and home rhythms that define modern life, securing this rest, recovery, and mental reserve can be difficult. We can all get better at it.

Rhythm

The third level is to build your attention and focus as you would build muscle strength. You must practice deliberately and persistently over long periods of time. The benefits of deep focus are profound:

- The agitated mind of distress becomes quiet and peaceful.
- You will sleep deeper and longer.
- Impulsive desires and addictions will subside.
- Your productivity on a task can increase up to five-fold.[54]
- The experience of deep focus is rewarding.
- Your relationships will improve.

Convinced yet? Good! To get started, choose the exercise and the equipment. Plan work and life in defined bursts of focus. If your goal is to write a proposal, remove all distractions, give yourself a set time and focus fully on completion. Always have a recovery or reward in place for completion. *When I am done writing this proposal, I will take a 15-minute stretch break outside in the garden.* Then move on to the next task. This is work rhythm.

At the end of the work day, refresh so that you can give loved ones your full attention. Focus on being fully present and engaged with their experience of the day. And for heaven's sake—actually, for the sake of yourself and your family— don't have a device in your hands when you do so. Listen. Pay attention. Ask questions. Reflect. Make eye contact. Smile. Give hugs.

When you pick up a book, resolve to give a chapter full focus through to completion. Many read a few lines, check social media and go back to the beginning. Interrupted reading is far less fulfilling and certainly will not support learning.

As work is increasingly done at home, we must manage the boundaries so that we can complete tasks and connections. This is an important conversation to have with those who share your home. The Buddhists have a saying: "When you eat, just eat. When you walk, just walk".

Speaking of exercise, be clear on your goal and focus on the process without distraction. The typical gym is a distraction trap with loud music, multiple screens (often showing horrific news or violent shows) and revealing, bright clothing. If you like to work out to music, choose your own music. You can create your own "mix tape" with warm-up, intensity, and cool-down music you enjoy. I recommend you listen to music with neutral or positive lyrics, especially while exercising. Remember to stay focused on the experience of challenging and strengthening your incredible body.

Deep focus is exhausting but it can also be exhilarating. Be reasonable in your goals. Research shows that our ability to focus declines through the day.[55] It may be that you can only achieve ninety minutes a day of work with this intensity.

For most people there is a sweet spot in the morning. Develop a rhythmic habit of applying yourself to deep focus activities and allow the rest of the day to be a little more relaxed with meetings, reviews, communications, scheduling, and walking about the office or factory.

Meditation is the traditional way to build attention. Mystics, philosophers, and neurobiologists are all in agreement on this[56].Richard Davidson, an acclaimed researcher on the brain function, places attention at the centre of mental and emotional skill[57].

Over time we can increase our attention span and depth. Use the exercises above to work on this. If the average attention span for an adult is three minutes, the upper range for a trained mediator is an hour. Imagine if you could hold your attention steady and razor sharp for an hour. Your productivity would soar. You would find yourself deeply engaged in your life. Flow would emerge.

Think of your attention as a beam of light, generated by the resources of the brain (the battery) and directed by the conscious mind (the lens). Self-awareness is the feedback loop. Once you select the target of attention, focus the beam and dial up the brightness or intensity. Self-awareness allows you to detect the quality of your attention and alerts

Rhythm

you if your focus starts to dissolve.

Whether you are listening to a colleague or deep in meditation, it is exactly the same process.

Select the target, focus the beam, increase the intensity, and keep it steady until it is complete.

Your experience of life will change dramatically. Distraction, messy thinking, and attention deficits fade away.

Stay alert to the breadth of attention. At times you must drill into the fine detail such as a word, a movement, or mathematical figures. At other times, you must expand the focus to include more context. Leaves, branches, trees, forest. Once again, there is an optimal rhythm to mental activity.

To play good tennis, you must focus on the ball strike and then broaden focus to the court and movement around you. We can all master this skill of focused attention.

Drill 50: Select your daily attention training

Work or home tasks

Reading or study

Music, sport or hobby

Deep listening to another person

Attuning to nature: sights, sounds, smells

Meditation or other contemplative practice.

Situational Agility

Metacognition (conscious self-awareness) and focused attention can drive you down rabbit holes. You may be so focused on yourself that you fail to read others. Perhaps so absorbed in a spreadsheet that you don't notice an earthquake. When angry, you can be so focused on exacting revenge that you are blind to truth and creative solutions.

The final drill for your mind is to adapt creatively to real-world situations.

Most of us learn this through experience and practice. We try something, assess the outcome, and adjust until it improves. This is iterative or intrinsic learning. It works. The risk is to act on the wrong idea or leap impulsively. We act without thinking.

The alternative is to think through the situation, the options, and their probabilities of success. This is extrinsic and theoretical learning. It also works. The risk is to overthink a situation—a committee that takes three years to vote on fixing a street hole. We think and plan, ad nauseum, but fail to act, or we do too little, too late.

We all know people who sit on these extremes. The first solution to situational agility is to have a diverse team, play to your strengths, and pay attention to the input from your team members. However, to become an expert, it is necessary to apply and drill both until the skills of bold action (implementation) and thinking (analysis) are both strong. Then you can execute the right action at the right time.

There are three components to master:

- First, insight to your own state which allows you to map your body, emotion, and mind as you engage with a situation. We have laid these foundations for self-awareness.

- Second, flexible perspectives. This expands your point of view to embrace different ideas—how others may see a situation or less obvious creative solutions.
- Third, test different combinations to solve the problem. We can do this through mental models or through short, practical trials. We imagine how our approach and the solution fit the situation. When it looks promising, we test it. If the trial delivers results, we focus on execution.

This process allows for creativity. We create different states and approaches to situations. This is our unique human gift. It is a classic inside-out model. Assess and adjust your physical, emotional, and mental state (inside) and then generate different solutions to test and apply (out).

Drill 51: Nine steps to situational agility

Recognise when and where a creative solution is needed.

Map your current physical, emotional, and mental state.

Adjust these states to expand your view and creative energy.

Generate as many possible solutions as possible.

Analyse the benefits and risk of each solution.

Map out the process of execution for the most likely solutions.

Test these solutions in short practical trials.

Learn, adjust, and then execute the best solution.

Practise and drill the solution until you master it.

Dr. Sven Hansen

Not every challenge requires deliberate effort. Be selective and choose situations that are meaningful and deserve effort. Sometimes your body and emotions will alert you to important situations. You may feel tense, energised, or depleted. You may sense a feeling of anxiety, frustration, or sadness. This is the signal to dig in and work on it.

Immediately we can apply name, tame, and reframe. Describe your physical, emotional, and mental experience (name it). Step back, relax and take the time you need to generate curiosity (tame it). Imagine and evaluate how different states might help you (reframe it). You are creating the optimal performance state for the situation.

Physically you might get a good night's sleep, exercise, or energise your posture. Emotionally, you now have the tools to generate feelings of curiosity, hope, empathy, or appreciation. Mentally, you can activate optimism, focus, and resolve. There are many possible combinations that you can test and explore.

You are the creative organism. That means you need to be in the right state to apply creativity to the situation. If you can see where your state is lacking, you can now make the change. At times it might be as simple as sleep—particularly dream sleep. At other times, you may need to work on multiple elements.

The figure below provides a process to help you recognise where and how you can adjust your performance state. You get to bring all the skills we have covered thus far to this challenge. Once you have the mental model, you can get to work on fine-tuning it. Experts in all fields find ways to master their performance states.

	BODY	EMOTION	MIND	ACTION
MASTERY	8. What is required of your body?	7. What feelings/ emotions support you?	6. What thoughts will drive this?	2. Describe desired outcome
	Sleep Fitness Nutrition Posture	Emotional literacy Impulse control Emotional combat Altruism/empathy	Attention/Presence Noticing Disputing Reframing/visualise	Do what you love Get outside Daily practice Get a coach
INSIGHT	5. What is the effect on your body?	4. What feelings do you have?	3. What are you thinking?	1. Describe situation to change

Figure 18: Name, tame, and reframe your performance state. Pay attention to the sequence. First identify the situation to change. Second, visualise a desired outcome. Third, define the thoughts, then emotions, and then physical state that led to the situation you want to change. Finally, define the kind of thinking, then emotions, and then physical state required to achieve the outcome.

Once you have mastered your internal state, your mind is free to generate creative solutions. As your state and confidence improve, you will find it easier to imagine different ways to solve any problem. What looked hopeless transforms into motivating engagement.

In order to select good solutions, take enough time to generate a range of possible options. This is the beauty and synergy of brainstorming and teamwork. Explore the benefits in depth. The next step is to evaluate the risk in each option. This will shorten the list.

Take time to map out how each option might play out. You can do this in your mind. Or map it out into a process diagram with an old-fashioned chart pad, notebook, or digitally. At times you may actually need to try it, or a segment of it, out in a real-world simulation. This might be a practice session, a scaled-down model, or a computer simulation. In time you will need to test your solution in the real world.

Athletes, musicians, and stage performers run this process continually. Massive self-discipline goes into securing the right state. Performance is reviewed in detail. Adjustments are made and practiced. Thousands of hours are required for expert performance.

In family life, relationships, and business, we seldom see such deliberate and focused effort. Imagine what could happen if you put this kind of work into your parenting, significant relationships, and business operations?

Expert performance takes time. When a novice watches an expert, it looks effortless. They are in Flow. Then when you put yourself in the same situation, it is overwhelming. Think about your first date, your first competitive sports performance, trying to surf a wave, the first time you drove, or your first business presentation.

You probably collapsed your performance state. You become stiff and clumsy, panic welled up, and your mind froze. Many give up at this point. Experts reflect, adjust and try again—thousands of times. They have the benefit of coaches and video replays. With experience, review, and ideally with modelling and mentoring, they learn to master their performance states by recognising the best patterns and processes to follow.

What seemed like an overwhelming, rushed, and chaotic nightmare now becomes organised and spacious. The mind, emotions, and body are learning to notice patterns. These patterns allow you chunk up complexity which frees mental space. Reactions become faster. Biological errors reduce. Agility and creative solutions follow.

Integral Daily Rhythms

Now it's time to bring emotional, and mental growth into your daily rhythms. The goal is to explore, uncover, and follow a daily rhythm that helps you gain altitude.

There are phases in life when we lose altitude, phases of Bounce, and phases of exuberant fulfilment. This rhythmic movement up and down the spiral is normal. Ride these longer waves with equanimity and curiosity.

What you can do right now is agree on the key elements of a rhythm that stirs and stimulates the Bounce-and-Grow process. We have covered the details above. Start with your sleep routine, build in an exercise routine, eat consciously and healthfully, and set times to work on your emotions and mind.

Yes, you will have to make time for this and enforce discipline. Sleep and exercise call for resolve. These two are the big blocks that most people allow to slip. When you feel the need for a weekend sleep-in, remind yourself that this is off the table—it's not negotiable.

Always wake up at the same time. When your circadian rhythm is matched to your location and set in stone, every other function and rhythm will improve. Lock it in. Use the blue light of dawn. Cool down deliberately before sleep. When this rhythm is disrupted by children, travel, or work, reset it again as soon as possible.

Physical exercise is much more flexible. Yes, you need thirty minutes a day, but you have so many choices. Stretch, walk in the mornings, bound up the stairs, squat, work in the garden, dance, lift weights, do an activity you love out in nature, etc.

Be playful with movement. Remember that we are exquisitely designed to move.

If you can lock and load the combination of sleep and movement, every element of your life will improve—health, energy, happiness, libido, productivity, and longevity. Add roughly eight minutes of slow, diaphragmatic breathing to this, and your foundations will be very strong.

Life will throw you curveballs. Kids get sick, we travel, and work interferes. Protect your basic rhythms. Your life, literally, depends on it. I recommend three levels of cadence in your daily rhythms. In adversity, you slow the cadence. At other times lift the cadence and build momentum.

Set up a basic non-negotiable rhythm that you protect and maintain even in the most difficult times.

This is an investment of only thirty minutes in total. Are your health, wealth, and happiness worth it? I think so.

Drill 52: Basic non-negotiable daily rhythm example

Never compromise on your wake-up time.

Get blue light at dawn—even if from your device but preferably outside.

Stretch for five minutes with slow, extended breathing.

Squeeze in a ten-minute brisk walk.

Take a Tactical Calm break or powernap after lunch.

Engage in a form of play or laughter.

Be clear on one important goal that you will complete today.

Own this. Adapt your non-negotiable rhythm to fit your needs. Be willing to explore and test. Accept disturbance and fix it. There is no argument amongst experts on these basic practices.

When life is good, see if you can extend your rhythm to include more expert recommendations. Your are increasing your cadence. Energy increases. It feels great.

Drill 53: Normal cruising daily rhythm example

Execute your wake-up stretching routine.

Include 10 minutes of Tactical Calm or meditation.

Work positive emotions and focus on the present.

Do at least 30 minutes of moderate exercise.

Appreciate a social, healthy meal—breakfast, lunch, or dinner.

Set a ninety-minute period for deep focus on purposeful goals.

Take five mini-breaks to relax and recover—default mode network.

Allow for a period of enjoyment, play, reading, or intimacy.

Switch off all screens and blue lights at least one hour before sleep.

Relax, be grateful, breathe slowly, and sleep deeply.

Be creative. Find what works best for you. Make sure to hold the discipline for at least ten days before you adapt. Have a conversation at home to encourage your household to work on this together. Respect each other. Compromise. Keep your sense of humour.

You may want to stretch further and seek higher levels of life fulfilment or performance. If your aspiration is to be the best version of yourself, explore more challenging rhythms. This drives momentum. There are many options.

Drill 54: Peak performance daily rhythm example

If you are training or working hard, try extending your sleep time.

Alternatively take a daily powernap after lunch.

Be dynamic with your stretching and balance—yoga is a good option.

Make time for at least thirty minutes of meditation or focus.

Add a strength/resistance routine to your weekly exercise.

Add high-intensity exercise to your weekly routine.

Enjoy deep relaxation breaks at least five times per day.

Drop your carbohydrate intake and increase vegetables.

With guidance from an expert, consider fasting or ketogenic diet.

Find Flow in your deep focus work and in a sport or hobby.

Drill the more complex routines with a coach.

Use a coach or a training group to sustain intensity and motivation.

Laugh and play as much as possible.

Rhythm

Maintaining peak performance rhythms is demanding. It is wise to crank them up for a period of six to twelve weeks and then take a break—periodisation. Think of this as reducing cadence for a time. Particularly as you get older, the body and brain need this rhythm of *stretch and cruise.* Both are essential for elite performance. No one wins if you overtrain, get sick, or injure yourself. It is common.

Working with a coach is strongly recommended for peak performance. Seek a coach skilled in your area of expertise—sport, business, or music. Carefully monitor key biological signals like sleep rhythms, heart rate, breath rate, and heart rate variability. Take rest days if your muscle soreness does not settle within a day.

You will feel the benefit of a good rhythm by the end of the day. You may be tired, but you will be fulfilled. You will sleep well. And the next day you will feel way better.

The real power of daily rhythm is the microtraining effect over time. Little bursts of deliberate practice accumulate over time. Even within two weeks, you will be much fitter, more energised, and significantly more productive. Injuries will heal. Chronic illness such as diabetes, high blood pressure, and inflammation reduce.

It is never too late or too early to start. The best time to start is right now. Build your momentum. Work up the spiral toward Flow.

Next, we move on to the third part of resilience—Connect.

Part Four: Connect

The purpose of Part Four is to realise, secure, and enjoy connection. We can be tough and fit, yet still be miserable. Humans are a social species. We long for connection. That connection is not just to partners, family, friends, and colleagues. It extends to the wider community, all living creatures, nature, and the planet.

Your family, workplace, and community have rhythms of connection. We are connected to the rhythms of the seasons, day-night cycles, growth and rebirth. The lockdowns of Covid-19 have been a lesson on the cost of breaking down these rhythms. Mental illness, marriage problems, substance abuse, short-sightedness, injuries, and sleep disruption all have increased.

By now, you know how important the connection with your own body, heart and mind is. Relationships are compromised when our personal resilience fails.

When you are down the spiral, the biology of connection is shut down. When you fail to rest, your empathy portal closes. You become self-absorbed. When sleep is disrupted, emotional and social mechanisms are compromised along with your decision making and influence.

If you want a good life or aspire to effective leadership, this internal network of connections that we have covered so far is essential. If your personal resilience is compromised, your life and your leadership are fragile.

First, we address the motivation and practice of maintaining strong internal connections. We will call this self-compassion. Next is a workshop on empathy. We will explore how to read physical, emotional, and cognitive signals in others.

Then, we go through the practice of building influence. This is a main purpose of connection. Finally, there is a practical section on leadership and altruism.

Rhythm

It is through and with connection that we discover the joy of living, loving, leading, and laughter.

Dr. Sven Hansen

Self-Compassion

Self-compassion is self-care with a light, generous, and gentle touch. To maintain our standing and security in community, we must get on with others. When we fail and create conflict, we can be excluded from important relationships. In a hunter-gatherer tribe, this is life-threatening. We needed collaborative effort to survive.

Due to the importance of inclusion, we have well-developed social emotions. They alert us to risk and guide us to protect our connections. Embarrassment, disgust, and shame are uncomfortable feelings that we try to avoid. They motivate us to apologise, reconcile, and re-establish relationships.

When we lose connection, we may be harsh in judgement of our behaviour. This self-critical thinking can help us identify the problem and attempt to resolve it. However, overly self-critical rumination is deeply destructive.

We can sink into ever-deeper loops of self-abuse. We feel, think, and even say things about ourselves that we would never inflict on another. If we behaved like this to a loved one, it would be labelled abuse.

In a fast-paced, consumer world where appearances and performance are in the spotlight, self-critical dialogue can become a mental disorder. *I'm useless. I'm so stupid. I'm ugly. Nobody loves me. They must think I am such a loser.*

Be alert to behaviour that upsets others. You can carefully evaluate your errors. This triggers a desire to repair the upset—apologise quickly, make amends, and rebuild trust. All too often, we fail to take remedial action. Then we can sink into increasingly vicious spirals of self-abuse.

These repetitive loops of self-critical thinking can lead to dangerous self-hatred. The deeper down you go, the harder it is to Bounce, reconnect and Grow. Self-coaching is the remedy.

Rhythm

If the actions recommended in this book have resonated with you, you are moving toward self-coaching. Pay attention to your response to challenge. A self-coaching stance sounds like this: *I really could do this. I am worth it. This will improve my life. I* really *care about this. I can and will do this.*

A self-critical stance sounds like this: *I know I should do this. I mostly fail. I am lazy. Hell, I must whip* myself *into shape. But I know it is useless. I hate my life.*

My apologies if this is on the nose. The evidence is supportive. The way people answer the self-critical question in our resilience survey is consistently one of the top risk factors that undermine a good life. In our 2022 research, 100% of people in the bottom 10% of resilience scores are self-critical very often or nearly always.

Now you are identifying and naming unhelpful self-abuse. How do you build self-coaching?

Drill 55: Introduce self-coaching to your internal dialogue

I'm OK. I'm a good human.

I'm perfectly imperfect.

I accept that I made an error. I'm human.

We learn through our mistakes.

I am responsible and will apologise immediately.

I'm a decent person and improving.

Oops, messed up. Ho, ho, ho. Time to fix it.

The next step is to treat yourself like you would a child you love when they make an error. We comfort them, talk it through, and explore better ways to deal with the situation. Using an authoritative style of parenting, we help children understand the error and reaffirm good behaviour. With care and support, we set firm boundaries with consequences.

We progress from blaming and shaming to responsibility and appropriate remedies. Love for the child is reinforced. We challenge and focus on changing the behaviour. There is a difference in life outcomes when we shift from *you are a bad girl/boy* to *you are a good girl/boy, but that behaviour was not acceptable.*

Few people define and apologise for their mistakes. It is helpful to say: *I am sorry for the way I spoke to you.* It is unhelpful to add *I am a bad person*—even silently to yourself. Beating yourself up does no one any good.

An approach popularised by neurobiologists[58] is self-compassion meditation. It is increasingly accepted and encouraged.

Self-compassion is not self-indulgence. There are times to be kind and gentle to yourself and times that you must work hard to progress in the world. Once again, there is a rhythm to seek and to ride.

Drill 56: Self-compassion meditation

Take a relaxed, upright sitting position.

Exhale, relax your face, and focus on your breath.

Breathe in for four seconds and out for six.

Once you feel calm and steady, focus on your heart.

As you inhale, fill your heart with acceptance, compassion, and love.

As you exhale, let that kindness radiate within and around your body.

Maintain this focus on loving kindness toward yourself.

As you feel the love, let it radiate outwards to others.

In case you forgot, double down on your Bounce and Grow drills. The ultimate self-care is to execute your drills first. You care about yourself so that you can be a force for good as well as enjoy a better life.

Empathy

Empathy provides accurate information about someone else. Empathy is directing awareness towards others. Language on this topic can be confusing. Let's clarify our terms first.

Empathy is attending to and understanding the physical, emotional, and mental state of others. It is an active process of focusing the empathy portal.[59] This is made up of complex networks in the brain including the famous mirror neurons and spindle cells. These are discrete regions of the brain that process physical, emotional, and mental signals.[60]

Empathy helps us understand another person's experience. It is objective understanding. Empathy does not mean doing something for another person.

Empathic distress, which is also sometimes called sympathy, is the discomfort you feel when you witness the suffering of others. It can be so disturbing that you will do whatever you can to stop your own discomfort. While you may relieve your discomfort, it rarely serves the other person.

Compassion is active. It is built upon an accurate understanding of others and their needs. Think of it as desire that suffering stops and that others can enjoy peace, love, and joy. It can be simply an intention.

I prefer the term Altruism for skilled action taken toward both the reduction of suffering and the increase of peace, love, and joy. Altruism is the second peak described in *Lead: Be a Force for Good*.

We have moved well up the spiral now. Altitude is high. You are secure, energised, feel, and think. The foundations of your resilience and rhythm are strong. Your empathy portal is ready to open.

Empathy is biologically expensive. When we are threatened, it shuts down instantly. When blood sugar drops, sleep is disturbed, or we are distracted, empathy fades. The empathy portal will close in distress. It does not bother to let you know that it has checked out.

Empathy requires personal resilience.

Much of the good work done to build emotional intelligence, empathy, and better leadership is wasted on people who do not have the resilience or rhythm to receive the message.

To make sure that you can engage with effective empathy and constructive altruism, here are six steps to work on.

Step One is to take care of yourself as described in Bounce and Grow.

Step Two is to seek rhythm in human interaction.

Remember the person who simply cannot stop talking? There is one lurking in a coffee shop near you. Despite their companion's best efforts to contribute, they simply talk over others by raising their voice and interrupting. They barely come up for air. Is this you?

Please. Stop, pause, listen, and reflect during interactions.

We have strong desires for significance. Our needs, stories, and opinions deserve a voice and should be heard. At times, this pressure to be heard is so strong, we drown out the significance of others. Not only is the empathy portal closed, but the volume of self-importance has flushed the existence of others clean out of our mind.

Energy flows back and forth. This is rhythm and resonance. Ideally, a conversation is split equally between parties. When this happens, we have acknowledged the presence and significance of others. This is the rhythm of connection. Tone of voice—another rhythm—is also important.

Step Three is to focus the conversation on the other person. Be interested and curious in them as a person of significance. To do this you must still your own mind and desires. With curiosity and gentleness, ask them questions. Reflect back what you heard. *Wow, tell me more about that. That sounds like it was painful (or exhilarating or satisfying) for you. How do you feel about that? What would you like to do next?*

Step Four is deliberate focus on physical empathy. Start with bringing your full physical presence respectfully into the conversation. Remove distractions, direct your body and gaze toward the person. Give your full attention to their body. Notice their posture, head position, clothing, skin and eyes. What does their physical body tell you?

With skill, you can track a person's breath rate. Are they nose or mouth breathing? Accelerated, upper chest breathing through the mouth indicates arousal. Are they anxious, angry, or excited? Can you see the pulse in the neck? Is it fast and bounding, or slow and steady?

Physical empathy gives us an understanding of how someone is experiencing their physical state. This is the foundation from which we can build our empathy.

Step Five is to focus on the emotional signals—emotional empathy. Emotions are displayed in defined patterns through tone of voice and facial expression. These signals can be learned through Professor Paul Ekman's work.[61]

The basics include learning how to recognise the primary emotions of happy, sad, afraid, angry, surprised, disgusted, and contemptuous. The change in face and voice can happen in a fraction (0.15) of a second. They are accurate signals to what someone is feeling. It takes learning and deliberate practice to perceive them accurately.

Be alert to strong signals like sadness, anger, or contempt that might activate empathic distress in yourself. It is essential to stay calm and attentive. Use your breath.

Rhythm

In Step Six, we build upon these firm biological signals to activate cognitive empathy or perspective taking. We seek to get inside the mind of the other person. What might they be thinking? Based on the signals and your knowledge of the person, what is going through their heads?

Learning to perceive and appreciate different perspectives is one of the critical transformations for leadership, altruism, and civil society. Failure to embrace different perspectives leads to polarisation, relationship breakdown, failed leadership, and conflict.

Some are very good at this and know precisely the words forming in another's mind. Most of us struggle. It is perfectly reasonable to ask: *'Would you tell me what you're thinking?'* People appreciate your interest and will usually be glad to clarify.

Keep in mind that your foundations (steps 1 to 5) must be in place to do this well.

Drill 57: Empathy practice drill summary

Take care of yourself. Work up the spiral.

Monitor your contribution and seek rhythm in dialogue.

Acknowledge, respect, and show interest in others.

Be physically present and give 100% of your attention.

Identify and understand emotional signals in body, face, and voice.

Acknowledge and confirm physical, emotional, and mental signals.

Get to know the whole person.

In Step Seven, with respect and humility, you broaden and deepen your knowledge of other people's lives. Show interest in them beyond the conversation. Get to know their passions, important relationships, and challenges. This supports your empathy, builds trust and enables leadership.

A final reflection. To master your breath, sleep, or fitness takes effort but results are evident within days and weeks. However, empathy is something you need to develop steadily for years, even a lifetime. Take time to learn your basics as above. You will have to apply yourself consistently over long periods of time.

Working with a coach who truly understands empathy is worth considering. Facilitated support groups are managed to encourage empathy. Participants pay attention and listen carefully. They acknowledge what is said. Respect and altruism are built into the communication process.

As a leader, you can do this with your team. Take the drill above and introduce them to your team. Make sure you keep them alert to empathy.

This work is enormously engaging and humorous. Laughter is infectious as we guide participants toward better reading of their colleague's emotions. It is not uncommon to hear comments like *I had no idea I was missing so much*, *This workshop opened a whole new room in my mind*, and *That session changed my leadership and parenting*.

Empathy has genetic influences, but early environment is hugely important. Imagine the stimulus of a warm, open, and supportive parent and family bond as compared with growing up in a hostile orphanage. We must be respectful of these early influences as they will shape the expansion of your empathy.

It is crystal clear that you can take charge of this skill and build it over time. Tania Singer's research on empathy has shown that within six weeks of practice, empathy circuits function better. *Altruism* by Matthieu Ricard (reference 60 above) is a good guide to the detail behind this work. Essentially, participants who focused on physical, emotional, and cognitive empathy skills were able to show measurable increase in activity and volume of these empathy networks.

Now we move to a super-skill in life and leadership: Influence.

Influence

Collaboration is an ancient evolutionary adaptation that has enormous advantages. Even bacteria move together for protection or food.[62] Social insects, like bees and termites, are effective at dividing labour and managing extraordinarily complex work structures. A termite mound operates like a city.

Social animals collaborate and reach their peak in primates, elephants, whales, and dolphins. Leadership is a necessary component of these collaborative communities. We have a sound foundation through billions of years upon which to build.

In social mammals, leadership is sophisticated and critical to the success of these groups. Successful influence is the glue of leadership groups. Leadership transitions that disrupt influence networks can threaten the entire group.[63]

Influence is integral to being human. From the time we seek food from our mothers to our desire for time with grandchildren, humans seek to influence those around them. To achieve our goals and desires, the support of others can make the difference between success and failure.

A leader's job is to be good at influence.

They focus attention, understand the perspective of others, consider the long game, and systematically build networks. When leaders do this well, they succeed. And their followers are much better off, too.

When leaders fail in their influence skills, conflict escalates, groups break up, and the wellbeing of the community is put at risk.

The same rules hold for each one of us. If we can get attention, understand different perspectives, work on long-term outcomes, and build networks, life is satisfying and successful. Influence enables survival and is a key force for good.

There are two cautions to raise. First, history is full of leaders who have used influence for destruction. These leaders have developed Machiavellian influence skills. In most cases, they climb the first peak of self-aggrandisement. If they have empathy, it is focused on a small cabal of sycophantic followers. Their end is usually alone, violent, and tragic.

Second, in our social-media-obsessed consumer world, influence has become a digital science and art form. People and companies become influencers. Often there is no substance whatsoever. If you are liked or followed, being famous seems to be enough.

More sinister is the systematic, digitally enhanced promotion of products and services that ultimately cause damage and death. A current example is the Sackler family and Oxycontin.[64] Three generations of Sackler's mastered the art of pharmaceutical marketing and selected Oxycontin (an opioid pain relief) as their solution to the relief of severe pain.

The family made billions while millions became addicted to Oxycontin. They persistently underplayed the addictive risk of the medication. Communities were destroyed as addiction lead to abuse and failed lives. Hundreds of thousands died. As I write, the family acknowledges blame and agreed to pay a fine of $6 billion to US states.[65]

We must make a living. Many products and services cause potential risks to consumers—particularly if in excess over the long term. But humans have strong desires, a propensity for addiction, and short-term focus. Digital advertising can reach the most vulnerable populations and trigger impulsive purchases.

As we become more conscious and empathic, we become less tolerant of influence for profit at the expense of long-term wellbeing. Nevertheless, companies, politicians, criminals, and well-meaning individuals continue to spend fortunes on this kind of influence.

With influence comes responsibility.

Bill Clinton's *My Life* captures the immense investment a global leader makes in influence. Clinton's influence strategy began as a young man. His dedication to securing influence continued for fifty years. That alone seems a full-time job to me.

If you want to secure a job, get credit for your contributions, get promoted, work effectively in a team, or keep a family connected, how do you approach this vital skill?

It helps to be part of a functional family and community. Through experiences with extended family, early friendships, sports, and school, we lay the foundations of influence. Luck naturally plays a part. So does the desire to get things done. We marvel at young environmental warriors like Greta Thunberg.

Once again, take care of your Bounce and Growth. Dial up your empathy and pay attention to the structure of relationships.

The first influence objective is to learn how to get attention from those who matter. The world is crowded and distracted. If no one can see or hear you, there is no influence. Start with your close network of family and friends. Then work outward.

Take care of your physical presence. Look healthy and well. Prepare yourself and dress appropriately for the audience. Maintain an open and upright posture. Make sure you position yourself in the right place in the room or around a table.

Your physical presence shapes impressions in 40 milliseconds. If you are too formal and stiff, you threaten people and close them down. Yet if you look too depleted or submissive, you will be ignored. Present an open and welcoming posture: open shoulders and hands. This radiates warmth and trust.

Next, focus on strong posture and presence. When open warmth is followed by strength, people engage. If you show strength before warmth, people turn off. Get the timing wrong and your prospects of influence are gone. This is in the moment. As you advance your influence, there needs to be more long-term investment.

The second objective is to put aside your own needs and study the perspectives, desires, and state of your audience. Digital advertising exploits this. When you communicate, be sure to speak from the audience's perspective. Acknowledge their presence, their wellbeing, their feelings, and their position on topics.

Then, move on to create shared ground and explore how you might help them achieve their goals. Empathy is essential. It takes abundant biological energy to juggle between your objectives and those of others. There is a rhythm and cadence to this developing resonance. It takes years of practice to do well.

The third objective is to influence a person, a group, or a population to work with you. It will not happen in one conversation. You must plan, prepare, and lay the groundwork for days, months, or even years. We see this in great leaders. It is easily overlooked as it is so subtle and persistent over time.

Imagine you want to influence your manager to give you a promotion. Your influence work starts months before you pose the question. Get to know your manager's aspirations. Find out from colleagues how you think she might respond. Invest in working to meet this manager's objectives. Demonstrate your capability and motivation in the months prior to making your case to her.

When you feel a strong urge to make your case and influence someone, ask yourself: Is the time right? If your direct influence plan is not complete, pause, listen carefully, and bide your time. Once again, you are attuning to the rhythm of influence. There's an optimal time to listen, a time to pause, and when the right situation presents, a time to act with confidence.

This component of influence is as important in a marriage, with children, and in academia, as much as in global leadership. Perhaps it is more important to master your influence in your closest circles so that your base is strong. When a family breaks up in conflict, it can have a devastating effect on your ability to influence at work.

Objective four in your influence development is more relaxing in some ways. Here the focus is to build your support networks over long periods of time. Aspiring chimpanzee leaders are good at this. They grant favours, giving food, grooming, and protection to key members of the troop that they will need when the time is right to replace an older leader.

There are different networks that you can define and develop. Social media networks are trivial in that you may have thousands of followers but when you need something, all you receive is silence.

Personal networks are your real foundation: family, friends, and neighbours.

All too often, leaders I work with neglect these vital foundations. When something goes awry at work, they can be left floundering. Do not take your innermost network for granted.

Business and professional networks come next. These are the people you work with through your career. They may be friends, supporters, clients, colleagues, experts, mentors, or coaches. As we move into more flexible work patterns, we are learning how to balance virtual and in-person connection time. Virtual meetings can, if used well, save you a huge amount of time, money, and travel.

Strategic networks ice the cake for high-impact influence.

They require creativity, persistence, and deliberate efforts over long periods of time. For example, when you meet a new graduate at their first job, consider the possibility that they may become a CEO or politician. Could they be an important supporter in thirty years? Build the relationship.

As you shape your career or life mission, consider who you might need by your side. Where are the experts and communities who are leading in current thinking and practice? To strengthen your case, seek out experts with conflicting views. Know your opponents and keep your mind open.

Stretch your thinking into complementary fields. Many future innovations and global solutions will come from integrating different fields of expertise. Be careful not to go too deep into one specialty. Build relationships and share your thinking with people proven in different fields.

Drill 58: Practices to build your influence

Double down on your foundations and rhythm.

Learn how to get the attention in a busy, distracted world.

Understand your audience and communicate from their perspective.

Plan for long-term, indirect influence initiatives for big change.

Build your network of supporters and collaborators systematically and strategically.

Many have found it amusing to see how epidemiologists have emerged from a century of obscurity to rise into positions of influence through Covid-19. Timing and situations are often a matter of luck. Stay alert for your opportunity.

Influence is a wonderful playground in which to explore the rhythms of Bounce, Connect, Grow, and Flow. It is a high-energy investment. With your basic influence plan in place, the world will expect great things from you.

Finally, be humble. To influence effectively, particularly in testing times or conflict is demanding. Your foundations must be strong.

Coaching, in my experience, is essential to advance your skill.

Rehearsal, as a musician or athlete knows, is required. Working with a coach, you can frame up the situation you want to influence and practice the process. Repeating elements of an anticipated dialogue with a coach will make the actual execution so much easier.

Take small steps. They will be rewarding. You will have to work at this over long periods of time.

Next, we move into the goal of influence which is altruistic leadership—the kind of leadership our world most desperately needs.

Altruistic Leadership

Our final chapter in *Part Four*, asks what you will do with your resilience and rhythm. Do you want to climb the first peak of personal power and be adored? If this is your goal, get to it. Altruism and leadership are not important for now.

Or will you take your learnings from this adventure to be a force for good? Doing good work—helping others, saving the planet, and taking responsibility to lead others—is demanding and difficult. Whilst what is needed seems obvious, leading others on a journey of meaningful change will test you.

Altruism is the application of your skills and experience to improve the experience of others. It ranges from saving lives and comforting those in distress to creating conditions that allow others to flourish. It may even be coaching a world-class athlete or team.

Altruistic leadership demands self-awareness, humility, self-mastery, and empathy. It is easy to throw money or comfort at suffering. To effect long-term positive change is more challenging than good parenting. You have some control over your children. Protecting rhinos from poachers is a whole different level of complexity, risk, and trade-offs.

The beauty of altruism is the variety of options to do good. If you see litter on the beach, pick it up. Small thing, big smile. One can simply show respect and interest as you pass a stranger. There are no limits. Humble ideas have launched organisations making a real difference to people and planet.

While some leaders have the structural support and formality of an organisational position, even a free-wheeling altruist can lead a movement. Perhaps the only clear distinction is that some corporate leadership roles specifically target shareholder value or other internal measures. Altruism toward other communities and the planet is not necessary.

Dr. Sven Hansen

As the world evolves and many of us are becoming more conscious and empathic, altruism has become integral to modern leadership. Culture surveys, engagement, upward feedback, Environmental, Social, and Governance (ESG) goals, diversity, and equity-sharing are examples.

Leadership without altruism is falling out of favour. Consider the global outrage over Putin's actions in the Ukraine as I write this in March 2022. If we are to make it as a species through the challenges of our time, altruism is required. Leadership without altruism has been, is, and will be our greatest threat.

The popularity of New Zealand's Prime Minister, Jacinda Ardern, is based on her explicit commitment to kindness (or altruism). The world is ready for more altruistic leadership.

There is a risk for leaders when altruism slips into impulsive sympathy. We want to be generous, and at the same time build skill and resourcefulness. If we give away too many benefits, entitlement and dependency can undermine constructive outcomes. Altruism needs clear thinking and skill. This is the leadership of tomorrow.

Whether you keep your local park tidy or lead an alternative-energy enterprise, the foundations of altruistic leadership are the same. Life presses upon us with confusion, selfishness, and dependency.

If you want to lead or be a force for good, work this triad to counter those pressures: Direction, Support, and Autonomy.

Altruistic leadership broadcasts a destination. Direction is communicated clearly in words and action. Whether you focus on a tidy park or zero carbon, it matters not. We hear it, we see it, and we want it too. Direction also points to purpose and vision. You must know what is important enough to send such a clear directional signal out into the world. Take a stand for what you believe in and direct resources to create change. Elon Musk is masterful at this.

Rhythm

Support is the magic of human evolution. Parents, family, and community support children while they acquire the skills to survive and thrive. Support includes encouragement, space, and safety. In this 'coaching arena', children develop their skills and confidence.

Within organisations, leaders can provide this 'coaching arena' for employees to grow skills and confidence. With skills and confidence in your team, leaders can delegate and increase the impact of their teams. Others can apply their skill to the challenge and become productive. Support is not dependency. Creating dependency may feel good temporarily, but it will undermine the prospects of those you support. This drives a downward spiral.

Autonomy is the ultimate goal of Support. When we help others develop skills, they can support their own lives and contribute positively and more independently as well as interdependently and synergistically, which continues the upward and outward positive expansion spiral.

Parenting, teaching, coaching, and leadership all seek to develop the skills for others to thrive. This is autonomy. A student lands a job on graduation. Your athlete wins a competition. Your employees are free to get on with the job.

Every element we have covered in this book so far is exponentially more important when you step into leadership.

Leadership is a megaphone, a multiplier, and a magnet.

As we said at the start, leadership is the opposite of depression. Keep working on your altitude. Self-compassion, humility, empathy, and influence are the critical competencies to secure your leadership and use your position to do good and inspire others to do so too.

Dr. Sven Hansen

Leadership Traps

What can get in the way of us stepping up and serving as altruistic leaders? The relentless pressure of a leadership role with the added complexity of altruism can blunt your balance and rhythm. It is hard to see the change as you face one demand after another. The immediate dramas overwhelm your altitude. You can find yourself well down the spiral before you recognise a problem. Understand the following traps and tips for avoiding them, as you prepare for your leadership journey:

Death Spirals

This is the most serious trap. Forgive the emotive language. The term comes from insurance. When premiums and costs rise to a point that healthy individuals leave the insured pool, it leads to collapse of the insurer.

For leaders, it is a slow, imperceptible spiral down into *Resilience Failure*. You are so busy and driven that self-awareness and self-compassion fail.

Your rhythm fails first, presenting as sleep disturbance, missing your fitness sessions, no time for relaxation, conflict with loved ones, and persistent work problems.

You may notice that joy has disappeared. You are tired. You will find yourself in persistent bouts of anxiety (Flight), frustration (Fight), or despair (Freeze).

Because of your inner strength and grit, you will almost certainly press on. But your resilience bucket is drained. Your efforts are increasingly ineffective. Leaders often mistake resilience for grit. Grit cannot help you recover.

Your personal resilience is failing, and you're losing altitude. You are sucking on an empty tank. Pride and fear cause you to flail and get deeper in difficulty. You may develop health issues, marriage difficulties, conflicts in your team, and resignations.

Rhythm

At times, business failure drives leaders to seek help. Sometimes this comes from the board. The worst outcome is when the leader abandons the business or the job or even loses a marriage.

First principle: Never make significant decisions when you are caught in the downward spiral. You make bad decisions that lead to regret. Get yourself sorted out first. Then calmly decide what to do.

Second principle: With humility and courage, find someone to talk this through with. It may be a colleague, mentor, trusted friend, or professional. Connection, clear analysis, rational thinking, and support are critical.

Third principle: if you feel confused, disengaged, or anxious, correct your basic practice and rhythm immediately. If that requires that you take a step out of the swirling maelstrom, do so. You need rhythm and you need perspective. Step back, step up and step in.

Empathic Distress and Sympathy

In a more conscious environment, leaders are expected to show empathy, embrace diversity, and support equity. The cost of a perception that you are insensitive or uncaring is very high. Leaders are immersed in initiatives to demonstrate empathy.

Staying in touch with stakeholders and diverse perspectives in an organisational community is an added responsibility. Virtual meetings and remote work make it more taxing. Through 2021, leaders voiced the challenge with remote leadership. They found it demanding and exhausting.

Empathy reserves get stretched. There is the fear of being sanctioned for insensitivity. It is tempting to cross the line from empathy to sympathy. Leaders often mistake sympathy for empathy. Remember, sympathy is action to relieve your distress. Empathy is understanding so that you may be more effective in supporting the growth of others.

Dr. Sven Hansen

Adversity prevails as we transition from Covid-19 to inflation, supply chain challenges, great resignation, and war in Ukraine. People are battered. Their suffering will channel up to leadership. Real suffering, less face time and pressure to show kindness can trigger empathic distress.

Leaders can be overwhelmed. It is hard to walk the line between empathy and maintaining high standards of work. When you are distressed, it is tempting to drop standards and let people off the hook. I refer to it as compassion fatigue when this is ongoing.

The worst example I see is where a consistent high performer has a downward spiral. Because they are so "resilient", superiors fail to see the signs. They present from a doctor's visit with a diagnosis of depression or anxiety and a recommendation that they need a month off. It is awkward. They get sent home. There is no one at home. Work is their community. They get worse. Their leader remains ignorant. This does not have a happy ending.

Focus on constructive support. You must show that you care. Understand and acknowledge issues as process or structure that can be improved. Reinforce that you are committed to resolve the issues that are in your control. Tell the truth and be clear about what the organisation needs. Commit to a shared plan to solve the issue.

In the example above, make sure you debrief with the person. Apologise for not recognising the situation earlier. Commit to staying in touch. Ask what they need. Explore whether they would like to do half days or drop in to stay in touch with the team. Leave them in no doubt that you and the organisation are ready to help them recover, Bounce, and come back stronger.

As the world watches Zelensky and his team lead Ukraine through the brutal war with Russia, many wonder how much empathic distress they can absorb. While they are admired, how much suffering can they absorb? Is the world providing the support Ukraine deserves? Ukraine plays an important role in world food and manufacturing. Will we regret not supporting Ukraine more explicitly?

When we operate under adversity, it is doubly important for leaders to take care of themselves and manage that empathy boundary.

Decision Fatigue

As we step up to altruistic leadership, we confront our volatile, uncertain, complex, and ambiguous (VUCA) world. Building upon the foundations of Direction, Support, and Autonomy, leadership next needs to evaluate situations, explore options, apply creative thinking, and decide on a course of action.

Regardless of how intimidating the environment is, we look to leaders for hope, clarity, and decisions.

When leaders find their rhythm and cadence, this cycle of evaluate and decide builds momentum. Even if decisions are wrong, it is better to decide, move, and re-evaluate than to stay stuck and spinning.

Many leaders lose this rhythm. The situation is complex, the consequences extreme, and stakeholder demands are diverse. Leaders feel confused. They don't want to upset stakeholders. They stall on decisions. Everyone waits.

Climate risk is the worst version of decision fatigue. The consequence is that we become boiled frogs.

To avoid decision fatigue, leaders need an executive team and ideally a board of directors. It is the leader's job to engage and consult with these groups to thrash out the issues and find creative solutions. At the end of the day, the leader must make the decision.

Timing is critical. Restraint can save the day. The perception of procrastination spreads uncertainty. Trust can collapse quickly. If this becomes a pattern, leadership fails. Organisations rapidly lose credibility.

To avoid decision fatigue, ask for your team's support. Identify the risks of action versus restraint. Remind yourself that you must make the call and be willing to own it. That means a quick apology when you get things wrong. Learn from errors.

Decide again. Re-establish your rhythm and cadence.

Gossip

Humans love to gossip. In tribal environments, it was community news, normalised behaviour, and helped form coalitions. Social media has turned gossip into an industry. Senior leaders should be careful with gossip. It can undermine credibility and trust. The media lives by it. We drink from the fire hose.

The worst forms are coalitions (girls or boys clubs) that get together to manipulate a meeting or complain about someone afterwards. When you talk or complain about someone behind their back, you are seeding distrust. Those present start to wonder when you do it to them.

Appreciate others abundantly. Resist the human impulse to complain about colleagues. If you have an issue, bring it up with respect, honesty, and evidence when they are present. Preferably in private.

Trust will improve along with performance.

Distrust

For a modern society to function, trust in its leaders and institutions is critical. This trust has taken a beating. Can we trust our governments, professionals, medical system, and the organisations that sell us their products? Many think not.

The past decade has seen the failure of many trusted institutions. Consider modern media, social platforms, the 2020 US election, the oil industry, pharmaceuticals (remember Oxycontin), and even the failure of scientific journals to follow due process.

Trust is topical and, in my view, not well defined. Let's take an example. As a teen, I did competitive trampoline. It is an endless pursuit of height, difficulty and risk. One of the hard transitions is moving to double somersaults. To throw yourself into a rapid rotation at height requires trust.

First, you must trust the safety equipment, Second, you must trust your coach. Third, you must trust your own ability. If you cannot secure these trust relationships, you cannot progress in the sport.

It is much the same in any human enterprise. Basic safety is important. Leaders must demonstrate a clear commitment to safe working conditions. If reasonable safety processes are neglected, people get hurt and trust collapses.

Nothing in life is risk-free. Obsessive safetyism takes safety too far. It shows people that you no longer trust them with basic functions. Proper engineering is essential but forcing people to hang onto guardrails in office stairwells is almost insulting.

Second, people need to trust those in power. Honesty, consistent fairness, respect, and keeping commitments are the foundation. One explosive emotional outburst can wreck years of good work. People don't forget that one outburst.

Being fully present to each person is a powerful element of trust building. Some serial con artists present as strong and engaging but fail to keep commitments. These persuasive narcissists cause untold suffering to those who trust them.

Third, we need to trust ourselves. If I have a fundamental lack of trust in myself and my abilities, no safety equipment or coach will get me off the ground. This distrust needs more attention. With current levels of anxiety, hostility, and depression, many people are so distressed that their trust systems are simply not open.

This builds on *Tactical Calm*. When we react to life with Flight, Fight and Freeze, the biology and neurology of trust is not available. This is not because a leader or parent is threatening. It is because the person is in a state of threat. Everything feels threatening. Deer in the headlights.

Few leaders have learned how to address a traumatised workforce. The first job is to create conditions and learning opportunities that calm these reactive states. Perhaps this is one reason that resilience training has become so popular.

Just to remind you, if we apply polyvagal theory to leadership and culture, our first job is to help people find a calm biological state. When we feel that those around us are also calm, we have a biological capacity to connect with each other and extend trust. We build playfulness and creativity upon trust.

Resilience as Altruistic Leadership

Imagine a world where resilience becomes the foundation of family, education, business, nation-state, and the planet. Imagine if each of these institutions systematically cultivated the ability to Bounce, Grow, Connect, and Flow.

Imagine how we could turn the tide of mental illness. What if the ability to Bounce and secure a calm and connected state emerged from childhood and education to consolidate in the world of work. Depression, anxiety, attention disorders, and hostility would become something we can confidently overcome.

Imagine if we applied sleep, breath control, physical fitness, nutrition, and rhythm into our modern lives. This would further prevent mental illness. In addition, we could make a series dent in the explosion of diabetes, obesity, inflammation, heart disease, cancer, and dementia. We have the capability to save ourselves from preventable diseases that crush our health systems. These solutions are simple, readily available, inexpensive, and proven as detailed in this book.

Imagine if we cultivated emotional intelligence and mental skills. Imagine people being more self-aware, effective at self-regulation, empathic, and connected. We could rebuild families, communities, organisations—and resolve many of the unnecessary conflicts that rip our world apart.

What we have covered in this book holds the potential to transform our lives and our world in safe, inexpensive, and proven steps.

What could be more meaningful leadership? It is happening. Professionals and leaders at all levels of society are starting to address the theme of resilience. We see it in family therapy, in schools, at university, in business, in organisations of all types, and even in governments.

Optimistically, we are in a transformation with many tipping points. People are waking up. Leaders are paying attention. Many are taking action. Nothing is more important than altruistic leadership. We must fix ourselves, our families, our organisations and our society from inside out.

These are the foundations for Part Five as we next explore the concept of Flow and what it means to realise the best versions of your being and your life.

Part Five: Flow

Part Five explores how to push the boundaries of a good life. This is life operating in the top layers of the spiral. The experience is calm, energised, positive, and focused. The foundations of resilience are in place. With movement up the spiral, there is increased freedom. Choices abound.

There are many paths to live your best life. Thus, these chapters are shorter. You must become the master. This is your own script to write. Use experts and coaches to help you. Never forget you are the architect, author, and inspiration.

Here is where you realise your unique possibilities. With body (cart), emotion (horses), and mind (driver) harnessed, you can focus on the destination and the journey (the passenger). Here you discover the rhythm of Flow. Flow is your optimal performance state. It's where skill meets meaningful challenge. The magic of Flow brings out your own dance, enhanced success, and fulfilment.

The layers of rhythm from deep in your cells and physiology, layer up through your daily practices and connection with others. All the work of your journey comes together in Flow rhythms. Based upon these foundational rhythms, life develops a cadence or pace. From cadence, you generate momentum which becomes an irresistible force. You complete the rhythmic cycle of resilience.

Rhythm

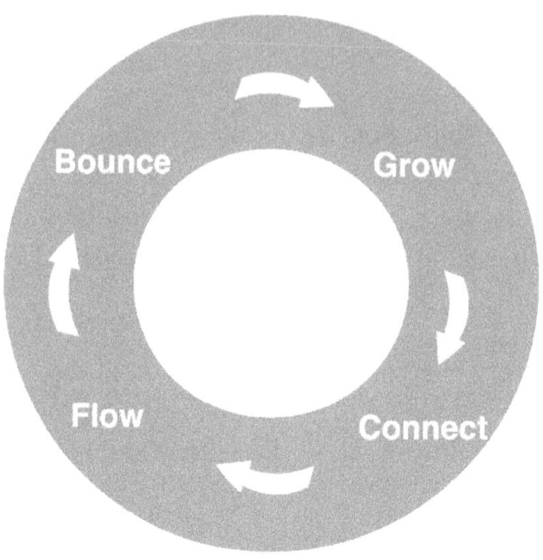

Figure 19: The cycle and rhythm of resilience

At times, adversity brings you down. You sense it quickly. Name, tame, and reframe. You Bounce forward fast, knowing that from each dip down the spiral, you learn and come back stronger, wiser, and more creative. You Grow, Connect again, and refresh your Flow.

First, I will describe how to build your experience of Flow and lock it in with deliberate practice. Next, we explore the role of purpose and *goals, building* upon the direction element of leadership. Then, Transitions stretches you to build your mastery curve and know when it is time to reinvent yourself. Finally, we explore how you can find the ultimate sense of connection. This is the experience of unitive consciousness—the goal of the mystics. Our test is to frame it for a modern world, so our connection is evidence-based, integral, and practical.

Flow States

From a biological perspective, Flow is the goal of evolution. It is optimised adaptation to an ecological niche. When you watch a raptor in flight, a leopard in the hunt, or a spider spinning a web, you feel a sense of awe. Generations of genetic experimentation match the skill to what is required to master the environmental challenge.

Humans are uniquely adaptive. With practice, we can master any number of skilled responses to tricky situations. There is no apparent limit. Citius, Altius, Fortius—faster, higher, stronger—together, from the Olympic motto. Witnessing people in Flow is the timeless attraction of the performing arts—theatre, dance, comedy, music, and sport.

Flow is the ultimate rhythm. It becomes part of your life once you master the basic rhythms of body, emotion, and mind. It takes a full tank and the momentum of rhythm. Flow is intense and demanding. Bounce must follow, which allows for Growth. Then we reconnect with the challenge to seek the next burst of flow.

Flow requires deliberate, focused practice over time. There are no shortcuts. It is hard work. The expert achieves Flow because she or he has secured the rhythms that keep them high on the spiral. They have mastered emotion and refined self-awareness, focus, and situational agility.

Flow is enlightenment. Flow leads us into the purest and most fulfilling expression of self. It is the purpose of this work. It is the call of your life. It brings us closer to God—or good. It gives meaning to the daily grind of your rhythm drills.

Life without Flow is tragedy.

Rhythm

There are many great books on Flow,[66] so I will keep the description short.

In Flow, the mind is as still and focused on a task as a monk in deep meditation. Thinking stops. You are one with the task. There is no doubt. Self-criticism stops. All available awareness, creativity, and execution are absorbed in the moment. There is no wasteful thinking, worry, or rumination. Your ability to track time drops away. There is a feeling of grace and wonder.

You are operating at your highest altitude. There is no mental illness or suffering in Flow. Body, emotions, and mind are harnessed, integrated, and co-ordinated in execution. Even bodily functions and pain drop from awareness.

When you match your skills to the right challenge, your productive or creative capacity expands. Whether it is an athletic feat, a creative project, or altruistic leadership, it is in Flow that you will *exceed* your expectations. You approach or hit peak performance.

At the same time, there is an effortless fluidity. A sense of calm even in the intensity. The experience is stimulating and even playful. Your mind or body is pressing toward peak, but it stays in the Flow zone.

Now let's look at two thinking traps that can derail your efforts.

The first is mistaking Flow as something genetic, a gift, or luck. The tempting explanation for expert performance is that she or he was born with the talent or fortunate in some way. Careful research shows this not to be the case.[67] Flow is the result of deliberate training over time.

You may be lucky to discover your passion and a set of skills early in life. You may land a great teacher, coach, or community of practice. Even the masters—Wolfgang Mozart, Albert Einstein, Pablo Picasso, Roger Federer, and Tiger Woods—trained and applied themselves for long periods of time under the guidance of skilled coaches.

Dr. Sven Hansen

You don't have to hold yourself to those standards. Flow can be achieved in a simple activity with an investment in skill development and practice. You just have to apply yourself to the task. As the task becomes more complex and intense, the amount of practice increases dramatically. Think in terms of thousands of hours or a decade of development.

Picasso painted for 80 years and worked through many periods and styles, accumulating a vast portfolio of skills.

The second trap is to believe you can optimise your performance for a full day. In business and parenting, this the default expectation. Abundant research on productivity shows that *after six hours, there is no gain in output.* Most of us flail at our jobs for way too long. In sport, you would collapse and injure yourself. In business, the signs are not so obvious so your eyes glaze over, your neck gets stiff, you wonder why it's taking you ten minutes to read one paragraph. Yet still, you push yourself. Enough, already.

Flow is intense and demanding. It demands careful preparation, strict seclusion from distractions, and deep rest afterwards. The rhythm is not negotiable.

Most of us work hunched over one device whilst pecking away at another device every three minutes. Our focus is fractured. Expensive switching of attention is almost continuous. One cannot get into Flow working in this way. There is no rhythm. It is madness. You will complete your day feeling exhausted. You struggle to identify one completed meaningful objective and wonder where the days and weeks go.

Flow is not traditional relaxation. Whilst watching music videos or sport or cooking on TV might engage you, there is no challenge to match your skills to. Flow demands a challenge. The goal is clear. You are 100% focused on how to achieve it.

Many clients complain that their senior leadership roles allow them little Flow. They remember fondly the Flow of being an expert in a particular discipline. This is common for professionals. Once promoted, they lose the opportunity to apply a lifetime of skill.

What are the practical steps and drills to build Flow in your life and work?

First, clarify what Flow is to you. Perhaps it is a deep expression of your unique attributes. Maybe the feeling of swimming or flying. There are endless dimensions to Flow. Search your childhood, look at favourite subjects, explore sports, check your hobbies, review elements of your work.

Drill 59: How to identify your Flow experiences

Search your childhood for memories of being at your best.

Ask parents, relatives, or friends from early in life.

What subjects did you find yourself deeply immersed in at school?

What sports felt good even if you weren't a superstar or even if no one was watching?

Where do you get in Flow in your current job?

What hobbies or sports currently engage you deeply?

Where have you built up a strong base of skills or experience?

Make a list of your physical experience at the time.

Define your emotions and the sequence of emotions at the time.

Can you remember what you were thinking?

When deep in Flow, your mind is so absorbed that your memory is impaired. There is no resource left over to organise the formation of memories. The combination of quiet mind and time distortion play a role. Reflect on the feeling experience. Reviewing a video or audio recording of the activity, or reading a journal entry you wrote about the experience, may be necessary for reflection and learning.

Recognising Flow in your past gives you an indication of where it might be in your future. It will challenge you to search your current life and job for Flow. If you have Flow now, wonderful. Deepen it. If not, accepting that your current life is not delivering enough Flow is uncomfortable. Use the discomfort to correct the problem.

Second, resolve to establish, rediscover, or deepen Flow in at least three core areas. Start with your own recreation, whether sport, hobby, or passion. This is the easiest one as you have full control. It will become your life energiser.

Next is your work. Remember that just ninety focused minutes a day is a great start. For most people this is in the morning. Others work best at night. Set humble goals. Single-minded attention on a repetitive task like data entry can get you started. The sooner you start on this work challenge, the more fulfilling your career will be.

This simple investment of thirty to ninety minutes in deep Flow work is one of the most appreciated changes for our clients. Locking in that Flow has a transformative effect on both productivity and leadership fulfilment.

Many professionals I work with have become deep experts; this attracts increasingly challenging jobs. Their career becomes rich in Flow experiences. Their next step is to take responsibility for coaching their direct reports and teams into Flow. Ultimately, this is the purpose of good leadership—to help your people discover and work in Flow.

The most interesting area is in relationships. Do you get Flow with your life partner? Whom do you experience Flow with? What are the social activities that build Flow? Couples might discover Flow in playing a game like bridge, in nature, exercise, gardens, dancing, or renovation.

For a long and satisfying partnership, Flow is an answer. Susan, my wife, and I have found it in nature. We love our walking and climbing. Susan has become an expert photographer, and together we have learned ecology.

I also treasure connecting with my two brothers for Flow. We have pressed the boundaries of many activities for a lifetime of wonderful memories. With years of experience paddling and swimming rivers and oceans, we have well established sets of skills. Tackling big waves or paddling in a heavy downwind swell quickly generates Flow experiences. It is wonderful to be able to share it.

Build your Flow into your weekly diary. Ideally, Flow should be in every workday. Even if just thirty minutes. Sports and hobbies perhaps twice a week. Make sure there is enough stretch and difficulty. Likewise in relationships. You are building momentum.

When you are an expert, you can make it up as you go. In the early days, structure is essential. Define the overall goals and the objectives. Identify the specific skills or themes you will focus on. Start with thirty or sixty minutes. Work up to ninety minutes as you find the rhythm.

When Flow is an integral part of your life, you will find both rhythm and spaciousness. Flow delivers results. It also demands rest. It is so fulfilling that you desire time to relax, read, or reflect. You will feel the intensity and reward of Flow as much as you will enjoy and treasure the quieter times.

Finally, be patient. ***Flow takes time***. Identifying the right challenges and developing a base of skills to match them requires sustained application. There is no harm in trying something and ruling it out. In fact, if you are currently thinking that you don't have much Flow, brainstorm a list. Get started on one today.

Once you identify the challenge—for example, to design a new product, learn to swim, play guitar, or become a birdwatcher—it is wise to engage with a good mentor or coach to accelerate your learning and mastery.

Alternatively, join a group that can support you.

Never be sloppy or lazy. Even when you're an established expert, approach Flow activities with focused attention, curiosity, and precision.

As a teacher, leader, or parent, nudging towards Flow is your first responsibility. Maintain playfulness amidst the seriousness of learning and work. Play is a safe space to practice. Create those safe places and times. Encourage curiosity and risk taking. Be there to support with calm and empathy.

Remember that Flow is the goal of evolution.

We all exist in a niche. This is the ecological, social, and physical space you occupy. It produces certain challenges. To survive and thrive, we must find ways to meet those challenges. That requires skill. Choose your environment carefully. Not every niche will work out for you. Define the challenges you will accept. Perfect your skills. Enjoy the rhythm.

Flow requires a clear goal, so now we turn to the role of purpose.

Purpose

Your primary purpose as an organism is to survive, and, if fortunate, to reproduce and thrive. Billions of years of evolution produce an exquisitely evolved homo sapiens.

Rhythm and resilience are crafted into every component and process.

Pain will alert you to survival threats. Frequently it will trigger the Flight, Fight, and Freeze reactions to protect you. Pleasure and joy will signal success and wellbeing. You are a pleasure-seeking hedonist.

Without consciousness, mammalian designs organise purpose between these extremes of pain and pleasure. The basic drives—hunger, sleep, safety, sex, and connection—keep us on purpose. With consciousness, we can add the layers of self-awareness, creativity, and planning to expand the range and magnitude of purpose.

Consciousness increases as we move up the spiral. When our rhythms of Bounce, sleep, movement, emotion, mind, and influence are in place, we increase the power of intentionality and purpose. Purpose, like influence, leadership, and Flow, is a high-altitude human function. These are all biologically expensive and depend on strong foundations.

When our rhythms of resilience are compromised, energy is diverted to survival. Pain is prevalent. We are governed by impulsive drives. These cravings to reduce pain obliterate the higher functions of purpose. The next meal, drink, or dopamine hit becomes the short-term goal without conscious choice.

When in the lower layers of avoid, attack, or collapse, the body is captured by primitive reactions. The conscious mind is not available. This is where your Bounce drills kick in. The understanding and drills we have worked on can be activated. Your purpose is to Bounce.

Suicide is a failure of the survival purpose. The rhythm of resilience is broken. Physical, emotional, or mental pain is the dominant experience. It is common in severe depression. The work of resilience comes first and foremost to prevent and reduce the risk of suicide. The world is united on this altruistic purpose.

Active rhythms of Bounce, Grow, Connect, and Flow will open your mind to refining your purpose. Finding purpose is difficult. Clarifying what it means for you can take years. Putting together a plan, influencing those you need to work with, and pursuing the plan can be a life's work. Be patient and persistent with purpose.

Purpose is personal. It is a true domain of freedom. Purpose is the directional element of leadership. We must all follow in some ways. We weave our lives around family, community, business, and national boundaries. The rest is pure freedom.

Your purpose shapes this freedom. As you come to recognise what matters to you, distractions drop away. Purpose may become all-consuming. Some devote their lives to a grand purpose, sacrificing health, family, and leisure. Others will devote their lives to health, family, or leisure with no grand purpose. Perhaps the latter is the grand purpose, or perhaps balance is ideal. Only you can decide.

Drill 60: Questions to help you shape your purpose

What are your basic needs in health, relationships, and leisure?

What are your requirements for Bounce, Grow, Connect, and Flow?

What sort of rhythm will create the momentum you seek?

Where and how do you want to live?

What type of environment and community do you need?

How important is family and lifelong partnership?

What is your career goal—what and whom will you work for? Why?

Can you define a greater purpose beyond your job and life?

Who will benefit from the commitment you make?

Can you develop the requisite skills and influence to achieve it?

Do you have a Plan B if this one does not work out?

While it might be great to be an explorer in the eighteenth century, our current world is the ultimate playground for purpose. The consciousness, altruism, and connectedness of our time allow for limitless creativity. Modern tools allow us to understand the most complex matters and adopt global best practices. With the right message delivered in the right way, we can raise an army of supporters anywhere in the world.

We face a raft of existential challenges—nuclear error, climate change, biodiversity, diseases, environmental destruction, pandemics, and conflict. The next hundred years may be difficult. We expect fires, storms, floods, droughts, and food shortages more frequently.

The slow, boiled frog effects of carbon, temperature, ocean acidity, polluted air and water, and preventable disease continue. They are less dramatic but over time push us through critical thresholds.

We are wrecking the planet's Goldilocks period. Goldilocks refers to the wonderful stability of our Planet Earth. For millions of years, it has operated between comfortable limits allowing for life, growth, and environmental resilience. This stable support for life, referred to as the Goldilocks period, is nothing short of a miracle. Without it, life would be compromised. We show stunning disrespect for this stability. We are ripping the system apart. The damage already done will haunt us for a thousand years.

Part of your purpose may be to survive these threats. You may decide to tackle one. Or multiple. Your purpose might be humble or grand. Either way, there is lots to do. When I look at my children, the immediacy and enormity of these challenges feels very personal. Jamming my head back in the sand becomes less tenable.

A final theme in this chapter, which is yours to write and execute, is whether you will fight. If you choose to fight, what will you fight for? Social media is full of opinionated and angry groups determined to do battle. Yet in many cases, it is unclear how they come to their conclusions and what they hope to achieve. I recommend surrounding yourself, both online and in person, with positive, intelligent, caring people who can clearly identify and collectively move toward their mission.

We are leaving a period of complacency. Since the end of the second world war, we have given our trust to powerful groups including governments, global corporations, medicine, finance, and economics. They act in their own self-interest. Even in the face of overwhelming evidence to the contrary, they continue to deceive, protest innocence, and spend fortunes protecting their profits.

Rhythm

We are withdrawing our trust. We feel deceived and hurt. We are angry. We want a fair playing field. We expect the powerful to be responsible. Some are changing, albeit slowly. There is a restless energy to accelerate change and give the future of humanity a chance.

When I watch Greta Thunberg or students protesting for government action on climate, I feel pride and hope. Should we take a stand and fight? After all, it is our lives, our children's futures, and the sustainability of our planet that are at stake. I say it is worth fighting for.

This is our home. We share this beautiful planet with a rich diversity of life. We have the capacity to be excellent stewards of life on this planet. I think we should protect it. Will you join us?

Due to the cycles of life, your resources and purpose will change. Next, we take a look at transitions.

Transitions

Life has stages. We can define them in many ways. Between these stages are transitions. What was important to you in school may have little relevance to your parenting or latter years. We change.

Our resilience changes. Our rhythms change. What matters changes. The world changes. Our purpose may also need to change.

Transition is the long rhythm in life. Because it is so long, many fail to detect the cues for transition. This can lead to uncomfortable mismatches between who we are, what the world needs from us, and what we do.

Purpose requires intensity and focus. Major objectives require discipline and delayed gratification as we put other elements of life on hold. When a purpose has your full attention, the next stage of your life may be neglected.

For example, young professionals can be so focused on work that they fail to recognise the needs of their children and family. They miss out on the precious privilege to raise a family. For many, the opportunity is lost for good.

Also, many midlife people become so obsessed with work that they fail to take care of their health. Some hang on to their work and career long after it would have been wise to hand it over to a younger team and scale down their work hours.

There is a healthy tension between purpose and necessary transitions. Again, you are free to select your path. Faced with a sudden existential threat, we plough all resources into survival. As I write, the world is watching Ukrainians fighting for survival. Many treasured purposes have had to be abandoned.

Most of our transitions are subtle and may take years to negotiate. The example of planning for your succession as a professional or leader is a complex process. The right successor must be found. They will need development and coaching, and it should neither be rushed nor delayed. When this transition is successful, the benefits can be enormous for all parties. When it is sudden or chaotic, it can cost the business and everyone involved. Successful transitions may secure years of benefits.

In contrast to choosing a purpose at a point in time, crafting your life through its many stages, negotiating transitions and adjusting your purpose is a complex journey. Be prepared for surprises and adversities. Be alert for both external and internal signals. Stay in touch with your own biology and needs. Stay open to the needs of loved ones.

Most of us leave this planning far too late. A common error is when you sense the need to change your job or role. The drills below can help you reflect so that you anticipate a transition ahead. I encourage you to do these drills periodically. Set a rhythm for yourself to do this annually. Set reminders for yourself.

Smoothing the necessary transitions is well worth your time today. It will reduce future suffering and increase the potential for connection and flow.

As soon as you sense the desire to change, map your career out again. Re-evaluate your purpose. Test it for adjustments. At times you need a steady income to support your family. If family needs are a higher purpose, you may choose to delay a transition until security is better.

Over the years of watching thousands of professionals and executives, the vast majority stall too long. Fulfilment in the role drops. Strain and frustration can dominate. Conflict emerges. The transition can end up forced and disruptive.

Drill 61: Map your journey through the stages—adjust

Identify the main life stages that make sense to you.

Study the biographies of people you respect.

Prioritise what really matters, including work, love, and health.

View your purpose from each stage.

Consider the impacts on other parts of your life.

Reflect on how you will know that transition beckons.

How will you prepare for these transitions? When?

Be prepared for unexpected and disruptive adversity. Have a Plan B and a Plan C.

Far better to see the transition in advance. Proactively work your plan to negotiate it with respect, care, and resolve. Reach out for mentors or coaches if needed. If possible, start negotiating a future transition with your manager, team, and family well in advance of the actual change.

Open and respectful negotiation supports creative thinking that may lead to a constructive role change or promotion. This is preferable to a traumatic departure.

Committing to a life partner is another huge transition. Your single life will change dramatically. This is a transition that begs for deep dialogue. Understand each other's needs and negotiate the compromises that facilitate joy in partnership while leaving time to be independent.

The arrival of children is another tricky time of change. Time for yourself will vaporise. The joys of partnership will be squeezed. It is impossible to anticipate this disruption adequately. Many of the foundation drills you found so easy as an individual or as a couple will collapse. Sleep, exercise, romantic dinners, and hobbies may become a distant dream.

The transition to parenting is loaded because it is not just you. Suddenly, your loved one and the lives of your children are at stake. Whose career takes precedence? What are your respective parenting roles? How will you support the individual wellbeing of each other? What do you want for your children? How much are you willing to sacrifice for their futures?

Chaos can reign for weeks on end. If feels like a war zone. How do you have sensible conversations and negotiate when you are exhausted, and the kids are screaming? It is notable that during the 30s, resilience scores—particularly for women—drop markedly.

If you are blessed with raising a family, this transition requires deep and thorough examination and planning. While the joy of parenting is profound and meaningful, it will test you. Negotiate this one carefully. Take care of yourselves and each other.

In comparison, the empty nest once your children are launched is a completely different adjustment. It feels "empty" to be at home without the noise, energy, camaraderie, and demands of young adults. Many fear this emptiness and may negotiate to keep children at home. This is an uncomfortable transition but is necessary to move to the next phase.

The next phase if you are partnered is to be a couple again. Firstly, our data suggests that you will be at your most resilient. Sleep, exercise, romantic dinners, and hobbies can be re-established and are deeply satisfying.

Being a couple again can be a time of delightful friendship and exploration. You have more time and less economic pressure. You have wonderful memories to appreciate. If you are lucky, you may be able to afford to retire or reduce your hours. You will be surprised at how happy you become.

This transition has its challenges. Some partnerships have already unravelled due to neglect, parenting or work demands, infidelity, health problems, or incompatibility. The solution is to maintain the joys and rituals that you treasured through family life. As the demands of parenting reduce, be deliberate in building activities that you can enjoy together. Explore how you can create Flow in at least one activity as an older couple.

Some people choose to work into their eighties and beyond. If work is fulfilling, it makes sense. If not, we must transition skilfully from full-time work towards a new life. A sudden stop is not recommended. If that happens, be sure to have interests, hobbies, or volunteer opportunities idling in the background, or find new ones.

Part-time work, mentoring others, board memberships, or voluntary work can smooth the transition. The explosion of virtual and work-from-home options available to us today provide a wide-open space for creative expression in different forms of work or community engagement.

In the great circle of life, our vital energy will dissipate. While we can extend and enhance life, we must all pass on. Whilst this final transition will have its challenges, it is far easier if we can overcome the fear of death. This is important personal work. The medicalisation of death leads to an expensive, alienating, and frightening experience. We can learn acceptance. We can engage family. We can bring dignity to death. Atul Gawande has a beautiful book *Being Mortal* to help us negotiate this final transition.[68]

And finally, let's journey onward to look at what may be most essential of all: Life as love.

Life as Love

On the spiritual path, this is your only purpose—to be one with all — with God, gods, consciousness, cosmos, nature, life, and others. To be one means embracing all of which you are aware with the feeling of love. This is unitive consciousness.

How you name this territory is up to you. With an open heart, you simply feel an open, compassionate embrace of all that you experience. While you naturally feel loyalty to your chosen way, embrace different paths with respect.

Love and kindness are the opposite of anger and hate. Being one with all, you can only respect, care, and embrace all that you are aware of. You feel love toward your own body, heart, and mind. You feel love toward those around you, your work, and your environment. Your love can extend through all time and space to embrace the awareness of the universe.

Life and consciousness can arise only through your own awareness. For your brief lifetime, you are aware of self, others, and nature. So far as we can discern, when you pass on, you have no further awareness. Don't take this precious awareness for granted. Treasure it. Don't fill awareness with distress, fear, anger, and grief.

When born, you are one with mother and environment. This is primitive unitive consciousness. As we develop, you differentiate your own being from other people and things. You must know when you are eating your finger or your dinner. Humans must individuate and identify before we can unify again.

Separating our bodies, feelings, and thoughts is essential to creating a sense of identity: me and not me. The two-year-old is a self-centric little terrorist whose being is to want it all. There is little empathy or altruism at this stage.

As we reach our teenage years, the process of connecting begins.

We seek to connect with our family, our peers, activities, nature, and the world through learning. It is still conditional. *I love you, Mum, but only if I can have an iPhone.*

As a young adult, we may expand our connection to nature, threatened species, or human suffering. Whilst this can be deeply meaningful, protecting this connection with nature requires resilience. Others identify with online shopping, fast cars, rock stars, and influencer fame. At worst, we may connect with violent video games, weapons, and acts of violence.

As we become adults, we find it easier to embrace our family, our work colleagues, and our friends. We find a better balance. We have an in-crowd to love and an out-crowd to avoid. Concentric circles. For most, this is enough.

Some seek more. Curiosity drives you to understand the world around you. You examine, explore, debate, test, drill, and master. Maybe you find an established guide or methodology. Perhaps you must discover and define it yourself. The common catalyst for this quest is a sense of awe in nature. Awe is what you might experience in a magnificent sunrise. A powerful sense of connection arises with respect and humility. We begin to truly feel what matters to us—ocean, mountain, romance, community, sport, sky, wildlife, etc. It is limitless. This is nature mysticism.

Your sense of awareness has expanded. The boundary between self and other softens. You move from "I" to "we". You feel compassion to self and others. Tolerance and forgiveness grow. It is much easier to apologise. People irritate you far less. You relate better within diverse communities.

Then you find a way to embrace the drama of life. Yes, there will be storms, fire, war, crises, and awfulness. There also will be times of beauty, abundance, peace, and goodwill. You ride through the drama with more steadiness and equanimity. You will feel the drama, suffering, and joy but your sense of self remains strong, respectful, and altruistic.

Rhythm

When you are the calm in the eye of the storm, you become a beacon of light and hope for others.

And from this place, you can be your most powerful self. You are present, calm, in control, and connected to the reality of the situation. You are more intuitive and inspired.

The universe, just like you and I, is full of wrinkles and errors. As you reach more conscious connection with reality, you can embrace reality with an open-hearted love. It is no longer necessary to judge. We transition from *This is awful* to *This is.* We are ready to engage for the greater good.

> **Drill 62: Work up the layers of consciousness**
>
> Accept all layers as natural and normal evolutions of life.
>
> Be curious and interested in others.
>
> Connect with and establish your community.
>
> Explore your world: people, nature, philosophy, religions.
>
> Tune into your awe experience—broad and then deep.
>
> Practise non-judgemental compassion for self and others.
>
> Extend an altruistic embrace to the universe with which you are one.

Love is much easier when you are calm, energised, feeling, and thinking. When you sink into the spiral of resilience failure, love shrivels.

The journey to higher levels of resilience is the stairway to heaven.

Dr. Sven Hansen

Your rhythms make unitive consciousness possible. Here you find love, flow, meaning, and joy. There is no boundary. Love extends from deep within yourself to all sentient beings and the expanding cosmos. You experience that love radiating back to you.

When we achieve higher levels of consciousness, it is tempting to relax. It feels as if the work is done. *Surely*, you think, *now that I have achieved this sense of union with all that is, my work must be complete. I can just coast now.*

Well done. However, as every expert knows, you must remain humble and double down on the hard work that will sustain your journey. The work of personal and planetary transformation never ends. There is always another layer, another level.

Unitive consciousness is demanding. It is perhaps the ultimate athleticism. That is why it is essential to double down on your daily drills. Body, emotion, and mind must be optimised. Rhythms must be synchronised. The daily disciplines of every rhythm we cover must be maintained.

Some who achieve higher states start to take their mastery for granted. They become lazy. They become arrogant. They feel entitled to use and even exploit others. Many spiritual masters make these errors. When evidence of abuse emerges, the fall from grace is brutal. Be vigilant about staying modest and staying the course.

Your goal is to experience more of life as love or unitive consciousness. It is a powerful force. It casts a bright light. Others will notice. You will expand your goals. Be prepared to recharge the battery. It is very expensive to live in this enlightened state. While your body, emotions, and mind are much stronger, they still need deep rest and fine-tuning to sustain the good work.

We have much to learn about how best to sustain a life of love. For each of us the precise disciplines and rhythms may well be different. In our research on what distinguishes the most resilient from the most fragile, sleep quality, fulfilment, Bounce, relaxation, focus, and fitness rank at the top.

Drill 63: The daily disciplines of enlightened life

Secure regular, timely and quality sleep.

Appreciate and be grateful for what you have in life.

Master rapid Bounce and Growth in adversity.

Stay humble.

Be disciplined in securing your relaxation rhythms.

Sharpen your focus through daily contemplative practice.

Maintain a daily habit of building and protecting physical fitness.

The purpose of this work is to live, lead, and laugh. We do this from the inside out. We align the basic biological rhythms with our environment. We establish a secure state. Then we energise our physical resource.

With this energy, we are fit to engage feeling. When emotions are mastered, we access the power of mind. With body, emotion, and mind powerful and efficient, we enter the creative space of Flow.

Flow may be applied to your sports, your work, and your family. It can expand to the community around you, and perhaps even out towards the planet and our universe. Flow is being fully engaged without separation. In its most expansive and spiritual form, it is a state of unitive consciousness. Flow can be applied to a piece of music or to a courageous act of altruism.

As we close, let's review the Diagnostic and Development model again.

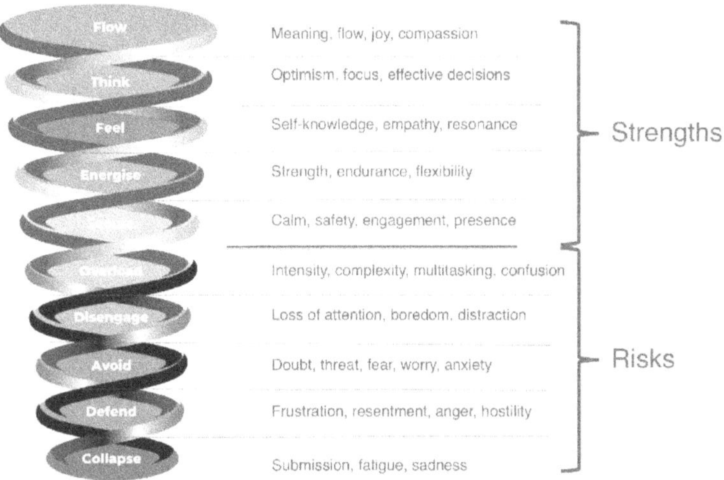

Figure 20: The Diagnostic and Development Model for Resilience, 2022

Life has altitude. At times, we soar to the heights of human experience. It is thrilling, rewarding, and joyous. Our resources are well trained and aligned from the basics of biology to the power of mind. We have abundant choice. Even in adversity, we are calm, optimistic, and agile.

Life at altitude has a rhythm of deep engagement, rest, and growth. We have mastered the rhythms. We execute with discipline and cadence. The joy we feel helps us to remember how to get back when we lose it. We will lose it—and regain it—again and again. Part of the beauty of the human experience is to be perfectly imperfect.

When we lose altitude, the mind is overloaded and disengages. Ancient reptilian reactions step in to protect us when the mind fails. At times these can be vigorous Flight, Flight, and Freeze reactions. They are shocking and leave us with regret. The body is trying to take care of us.

At other times in our frenetic world, repeated small reactions become embedded in our experience. If we are in a hostile environment with multiple small threats such as news, social media, e-mails, and difficult colleagues or loved ones, dissolution down the spiral is subtle.

Rhythm

Repeated doses of anxiety can accumulate into a state of fear. This is what happens in anxiety disorders. Repeated doses of frustration accumulate into anger. This hostility is the underlying disorder of a polarised, combative world. Repeated doses of disappointment and failure accumulate as sadness. This can lead to depression.

When we can see these reactions and states clearly, we can name them for what they are. They are normal reactions to threats. Evolution has protected these reactions. In our times, they are a liability.

When we can name them, we can tame them. As we tame them by making new choices and moving up our spiral, we feel secure again. Homeostasis returns to body and emotion. The mind comes back on stream. Now we can transform destructive reactions into fuel for growth.

With insight we can see and name each category as it unfolds. With practice we can master the next steps to move up the spiral. To really live, lead, and laugh, we must open the empathy portal and connect with others.

When we can connect with trust and playfulness, we become a force for good—a skilled altruist.

This is leadership.

Celebrate the wins. Laugh heartily. Acknowledge the downward spirals. Laugh heartily. Bounce forward again.

Time to take these lessons and drills into your own life. Continue the adventure bringing your passion, experience, and unique abilities into play. Find your own rhythmic Bounce, Grow, Connect, and Flow cycle. As you feel your rhythm emerge, add the pace and consistency that leads to cadence. Feel your life moving forward and upward. Nurture this momentum.

Drill 64: Bounce, Grow, Connect and find Flow

Dr. Sven Hansen

Acknowledgements

First, I would like to thank our clients around the world who have helped us define the challenges on the path to greatness. It is through thousands of hours working with you that we have made progress in sharing relevant and helpful guidance on your journey and that of many others.

A huge thanks to all of our team, who are steadily taking this work to the world. This is not easy work. It takes clear communication, strong relationships, courage, empathy and persistence. Through you, we have reached hundreds of thousands of people.

Thank you to all the professionals and coaches who have supported me on my own journey. Specifically, I am grateful to my parents and our family. We are blessed. School and my time in Pathfinders were wonderful times of growth. I treasure these relationships. Through medicine and the MBA, hundreds of wise and capable people guided me. Specifically, I appreciate the guidance and friendship of Dr. Merv Dickinson who has been a wonderful coach and mentor in expanding my view from medicine to emotional intelligence and leadership.

Writing is a long and testing process. I feel lucky to have found Sage Taylor Kingsley, who guided the editorial process. Thank you for your passion, humour, and wisdom in the field—as well as the detailed feedback and encouragement. And thanks to Lili Booth for assistance in formatting and preparation for printing.

Thank you, readers, for taking the time to understand and hopefully grow through the journey we have taken. In our busy lives, taking time to read, reflect, and plan is not easy. I truly hope you have taken at least one practical action into your future life.

Dr. Sven Hansen

Resources

Humans are surprisingly complex and diverse. Our brains alone rate as one of the most complex systems in the universe. Our bodies and emotional resources are wonders of nature. To really know ourselves deeply takes a lifetime of study and practice.

We have to learn how to work with these personal resources in a dynamic and complex environment and society. There are many paths to creating a good life. This book is just one attempt to create a practical guide to this journey of working from inside, outwards.

The following are recommended resources that may help you understand and master your own journey. Your own inside-out journey toward greater rhythm can be deeply rewarding and satisfying. You can create your life in ways that can lengthen your life, improve quality of life, create more harmonious family and social interactions, enrich your career, and transform the prospects for those you care about. This is a list of resources that might help you on your journey.

Bounce

The Upward Spiral, Alex Korb,

Lost Connections, Johan Hari

Polyvagal Safety, Stephen Porges, 2021

Breath, James Nestor, 2021

Polyvagal Exercises for Safety and Connection, Deb Dana, 2020

Rhythm

Grow

Self-quantification: we live in a time where it is now possible to track hundreds of your personal metrics from heart rate and steps to sleep and breathing. While it is important not to become obsessed with your own data, it is an excellent way to assess your starting point for Growth. Apple Watches, Garmin, Fitbit, Oura rings and many others can make this both simple and entertaining.

Perform under Pressure, Ceri Evans, 2020

Behave, Robert Sapolsky, 2018

Exercised, Dan Lieberman, 2021

Stolen Focus, Johan Hari, 2022

Why We Sleep, Matthew Walker, 2017

Connect

Altruism, Matthieu Ricard, 2017

Radical Candor, Kim Scott, 2019

The Age of Empathy, Frans de Waal, 2009

The Emotional Life of your Brain, Richard Davidson & Sharon Begley, 2012

Paul Ekman resources for emotional awareness and empathy: www.paulekman.com

Dr. Sven Hansen

Flow

The Art of Impossible, Steven Kotler, 2021

Peak, Anders Ericsson & Robert Pool, 2016

About the Author

Sven Hansen was born in South Africa, one of three boys in a family committed to a free and equitable transition. Sven's father, Emeritus Professor of Paediatrics, and mother, a psychiatric social worker, provided a dynamic encouragement to live by the emerging principles of preventive medicine. From his time at King Edwards School, Sven flourished in academics and sport.

Sven won an American Field Service scholarship to spend a year in the United States before entering compulsory military service. During this time, he qualified for Pathfinder Special Forces. He studied medicine at the University of Cape Town qualifying in 1986 before heading to New Zealand to work in Christchurch Hospital for two years.

He built up a sports medicine practice in Christchurch which provided the foundation for taking the science and practice of resilience to organisations and schools. In 1993, he completed an MBA, again at the University of Cape Town, where he met his wife, Susan. They returned to New Zealand to settle in Auckland and grow the Resilience Institute as a business.

Resilience was a novel concept at the time. As the business grew, his team integrated preventative and sports medicine, psychology, neurobiology, and ecology to create an evidence-based framework with practical applications. Based in New Zealand, the team expanded to include Australia, China, Europe, United Kingdom, South Africa, and North America.

The Resilience Institute is now a global business operating in seven languages with a well-established resilience diagnostic and a secure digital platform that supports thousands of clients every month.

Sven and Susan have two children, Lauren and James, and spend their lives between Auckland and Noosa. Sven continues to be an active outdoor athlete on the ocean and in the mountains.

References

[1] Koestenbaum, Peter, *Leadership: The Inner Side of Greatness*, Josey-Bass, 2002. In a complex world, Koestenbaum's framework for leadership is a powerful tool to keep your balance when leadership is complex. This was a life-changing book for me.

[2] Hari, Johann, *Lost Connections,* Bloomsbury, 2018. This is a deep and practical book on how we find ourselves in a mental health crisis with a rich resource of solutions.

[3] Kotler, Steven, *Art of Impossible,* HarperCollins, 2021. One of the best current books on Flow.

[4] Ericsson, Anders & Pool, Robert, *Peak: Secrets from the New Science of Expertise,* The Bodley Head, 2016.While a heavy and complex text, Ericsson's work on the science of expertise is an essential complement to the often hyped-up presentation of Flow. He expertly lays out the methodology of deliberate practice showing how expertise is sourced in practice rather than talent.

[5] Wu et al, "The prevalence of moderate-to-high posttraumatic growth: A systematic review and meta-analysis", *Journal of Affective Disorders,* Jan 2019. https://pubmed.ncbi.nlm.nih.gov/30268956/

[6] Werner, E. E. and Smith R. S, *Vulnerable but Invincible,* 1982. This is one of the most influential studies on Bounce, affirming that it is in reach for all.

[7] Resilience Institute Research, 2022, https://resiliencei.com/resilience-research/

[8] Resilience Institute Research, 2020. https://resiliencei.com/resilience-research/

[9] Sapolsky, Robert, *Behave*, Penguin Press, 2017. Our family loved this book. Sapolsky is well respected scientist who shows how our behaviour is based on physical, emotional, and mental habits. The biological explanations are among the best I know.

[10] Cooper Ramo, Joshua, *The Age of the Unthinkable*. Little, Brown & Company, New York, 2009.

[11] Haidt, Jonathan; Lukianoff, Greg, *The Coddling of the American Mind*, Penguin, 2018. To help us understand the limitations of safetyism, this book is a timely reminder of the importance of exposing young people to challenge.

---

[12] Seligman, Martin, *Learned Optimism*. Pocket Book, New York, 1998.

[13] Dweck, Carol, *Growth Mindset,* Constable and Robinson, 2017.

[14] Ricard, Matthieu, *Altruism,* Atlantic Books, 2015. This is a beautiful book integrating science and philosophy. Matthieu is a biologist and Buddhist monk who has been instrumental in linking Buddhism to modern neurobiology. A great way to introduce yourself to emotional intelligence.

[15] Seligman, Martin, *Flourish*. Free Press, New York, 2011.

[16] Ericsson, Anders & Pool, Robert, *Peak: Secrets from the New Science of Expertise,* The Bodley Head, 2016.

[17] Lieberman, Dan, *Exercised*, Penguin, 2021. Lieberman is a respected Harvard anthropologist and keen runner who writes beautifully about the importance of physical fitness and how it can resolve the preventable disease epidemic of our time.

[18] Gates, Melinda, *The Moment of Lift,* Macmillan, 2019

[19] Gates, Bill, *How to Avoid a Climate Disaster,* Penguin, 2021

[20] Bloom, Paul, *Against Empathy*, Vintage, 2017. While in my view, Bloom is writing about sympathy or empathic distress, this is a sound caution against emotional impulse without the guidance of wisdom.

[21] Lieberman, Dan, *Exercised,* Penguin, 2021

[22] Porges, Stephen, *Polyvagal Safety,* Norton, 2021. This is Porges' most recent book on Polyvagal Theory. Essential reading for anyone wanting to understand how to counter mental illness and discover how we can calm and connect for social engagement.

[23] Rosling, Hans, *Factfulness*, 2018. A wonderful book of hope showing how so many aspects of life are actually improving—even for those in the most challenged situations.

[24] Russell, Bertrand, *New Hopes for a Changing World,* George Allen & Unwin, 1951

[25] Bregman, Rutger, Human Kind, Bloomsbury, 2020. P 253.

[26] Grossman, David, *On Combat,* 2009. For those interested in the military applications of resilience.

[27] Evans, Ceri, *Perform under Pressure,* HarperCollins, 2019. Evans is a forensic psychiatrist who has helped the All Black rugby team succeed under pressure.

[28] Lieberman, Dan, *Exercised*, Penguin, 2021

[29] Hari, Johann, *Stolen Focus,* Bloomsbury, 2022. The best read of 2022 from my perspective. An excellent exploration of how our attention is

shattered by modern life and how to fix it.

[30] Baumeister, Roy, Tierney John, *Willpower,*Penguin, 2011.

[31]Shai Danziger, Jonathan Levavb and Liora Avnaim-Pessoa, PNAS

[32]*European Psychiatry*, May 2020,
https://www.ncbi.nlm.nih.gov/pmc/articles/PMC7355168/

[33]*ADHD Nation,* Alan Schwartz, Scribner, 2016. An alarming report on the prevalence and medicalisation of attention disorders.

[34]Porges, Stephen W., *The Polyvagal Theory*. W.W. Norton & Company, New York, 2012.

[35]Porges, Stephen, *Polyvagal Safety,* Norton, 2021.

[36] Dana, Deb, *Polyvagal Exercises for Safety and Connection,* Norton, 2020. Deb Dana adds a wide range of very practical techniques to apply Polyvagal theory in therapy and life.

[37]Twenge, Jean, I-Gen, M, Simon & Shuster, 2017.

[38] Lukianoff, G and Haidt, J, *Coddling of the American Mind,* Penguin, 2018.

[39] Hari, Johann, *Lost Connections,* Bloomsbury, 2018.

[40] Dana, Deb, *Polyvagal Exercises for Safety and Connection,* Norton, 2020

[41] American Institute of Stress, https://www.stress.org/daily-life

[42]Heartmath Institute, https://www.heartmath.org/ Heart rate variability is called respiratory sinus arrhythmia in medicine. The concept is much better known today thanks to Heartmath and modern fitness trackers. It is one of the best measures of vagal nerve activity, although there is much debate about the best way to measure it, as described by Stephen Porges.

[43] Nestor, James, *Breath: The New Science of a Lost Art,* Penguin, 2020. I love this book. Many of our clients have thanked us for the referral. It is interesting, entertaining, and very practical.

[44]Davidson, Richard; Begley, Sharon, *The Emotional Life of Your Brain.* Hodder & Stoughton, London, 2012 and Davidson, Richard and Goleman, Dan, *Science of Meditation,* 2017.

[45]These include some of the following well-respected academics: Richard Davidson, Jon Kabat-Zinn, Brian Hanson, Daniel Goleman, Daniel Siegel, Martin Seligman and Paul Ekman.

[46] Damasio, Antonio, Feeling and Knowing, Penguin, 2021

[47] Ericsson, Anders & Pool, Robert, *Peak: Secrets from the New Science of Expertise,* The Bodley Head, 2016.

48 Walker, Matthew, *Why We Sleep,* Penguin, 2107. A very popular and helpful overview of sleep science.

49 Lieberman, Daniel, *Exercised,* Penguin, 2021.

50 Goleman, D, Boyatzis, R, McKee, A, *The New Leaders,* Sphere, 2003

51 Damasio, Antonio, *Feeling and Knowing,* Pantheon, 2021

52 Damaiso, Antonio, *The Strange Order of Things,* Knopf, 2019

53 Hari, Johann, *Stolen Focus,* Bloomsbury, 2022

54*McKinsey Quarterly,* January 2013

55 Baumeister, William, *Willpower,* 2011.

56 Davidson, R, Goleman, D, *The Science of Meditation,* Penguin, 2017. One of the more grounded, practical, and sensible books on the science and practice of meditation.

57 Davidson, Richard, *The Emotional Life of Your Brain,* Hodder & Stoughton, 2012.

58 Singer, Tania,& Ricard, Matthieu, *Power and Care,* The MIT Press, 2019.

59 De Waal Frans, *The Age of Empathy,* Harmony Books 2009. A wonderful book on the power of empathy from a highly respected primatologist. One of my favourites.

60 Ricard, Matthieu, *Altruism,* Atlantic Books, 2015

61 Ekman, Paul, *Emotions Revealed,* Holt Paperbacks, 2004. This is an excellent foundation for understanding the primary emotions. It is well supported by Ekman's website where you can download a range of tools to build your empathy. www.paulekman.com

62 Damasio, Antonio, *The Strange Order of Things,* Pantheon Books, 2018

63 De Waal, Frans, *Are We Smart Enough To Know How Smart Animals Are?,* Granta Books, 2016.

64 Keef, Patrick Raden, *Empire of Pain,* Picador, 2021. Strongly recommended and horrifying story of how medical marketing can do tremendous damage.

65 La Valle, Lauren, "Purdue Pharma and Sacklers reach $6 billion opioid settlement",*CNN Business,* 3 March 2022

66 Kotler, Steven, *Art of Impossible,* HarperCollins, 2021

67 Ericsson, Anders and Poole, Robert, Peak, *HarperOne,* 2017

68Gawande, Atul, *Being Mortal,* Profile Books, 2014

www.ingramcontent.com/pod-product-compliance
Lightning Source LLC
Chambersburg PA
CBHW051049050726
47592CB00002B/456